Dyeing to knit

Dyeing to knit

**how to use
—and create
your own—beautiful
hand-dyed yarns**

elaine eskesen

Down East Books

To my children,

Robin, Eric, Dylan, and Emily,

who have taught me so much

ISBN (10-digit): 0-89272-667-9
ISBN (13-digit): 978-0-89272-667-7

Library of Congress Cataloging-in-Publication Data
Eskesen, Elaine.
  Dyeing to knit : how to use and create your own beautiful hand-dyed yarns / Elaine Eskesen.
      p. cm.
  Includes bibliographical references and index.
  ISBN 0-89272-667-9 (trade hardcover : alk. paper)
  1. Dyes and dyeing—Textile fibers. 2. Yarn. 3. Knitting—Patterns. I. Title.
  TT853.E85 2005
  746.43′2—dc22

All photographs by the author unless otherwise noted.
Design by Harrah Lord, Yellow House Studio
Printed in China

OGP   5   4   3   2

Down East Books
A division of Down East Enterprise, Inc.
Publisher of *Down East*, the Magazine of Maine

Book orders: 1-800-685-7962
www.downeastbooks.com

Contents

Acknowledgments

This book would not have been possible without more than a little help from my circle of friends.

A huge thank-you goes to Mel Fuller, who gave me the courage to start in the first place and provided encouragement and help all along the way. His knowledge and kindness filled many queries and unusual requests. Thanks, Mel. You know I mean it.

I also owe thanks to my family of knitters, who spent hours knitting the samples in this book and trying out the patterns one more time. The list is long, and I thank you one and all: Carol Aigner Bacon, Kate Braestrup, Karen Bragg, Emily Davey, Regina Davey, Cindy Flood, Ellen Gilliam, Sherry Hughes, Diane Joannides, Nancy Johnson, Kathleen Kennedy, Barbara Klein, Yvonne Lamoreaux, Linda Murdock, Lynn Plumb, Jann Schwabe, and Pam Staveley.

To all the knitters who have come into my shop over the years for a "color fix"—thanks for the conversations about life and the love of fiber that have ensued. We are a special group of people, that's for sure! Thank you for supporting my passion for dyeing these colorful yarns and wanting to learn more about it. Now is the time for you to do so.

A special thanks to Jann Schwabe for the many dinners I didn't have to cook and for all the help in getting our group together in the first place.

Sherry Hughes kept me in stitches with a continuous supply of good humor and laughter. We all need a friend like this when the times get rough.

My staff at Pine Tree Yarns kept the store going while I worked upstairs, away from the crowds. Pam, Sherry, Diane, Ellen, Joan, and my dyer, Lynne—thank you for being a great team.

Thank you to the staff at Weatherbird and to my friend Deirdre Barton for lending us clothes for the photo shoot. It's always fun to be there. Also thanks to Chris DeLisle at Aboca Beads for making the beautiful glass buttons shown on the Gathered Vest.

A big thank-you to our models: Emily Davey, Ian Kennedy, Mikayla Schwabe, and Caitlin Cass.

Photographer Nance Trueworthy was a trouper who kept the pace as we pursued our demanding vision of how to shoot the on-location photos.

Wonderful people provided us with their hospitality and the locales for some of the photos. Such hospitality is one reason we live in Maine. Thanks to Jackson at Stable Gallery; Jill, for her romantic haven; innkeepers Alice and Len (and owners Skip and Cindy Atwood) at Pemaquid Hotel; and Peggy, who has a great spot on the coast.

Thank you to Vicki Jensen, at Pro Chemical and Dye, for her technical support on this project.

The knitters and shakers in the industry need a special acknowledgment for their artistic contribution in the form of those exciting "guest swatches" on pages 68–70. Thank you, Pam Allen, of *Knits*, Rick Mondragon, of *Knitter's Magazine*, Jean Guirguis, of *Vogue Knitting*, Libby Mills, of Green Mountain Spinnery, Bill Huntington, of Hope Spinnery, and designer/author Prudence Mapstone.

Karin Womer, Senior Editor at Down East Books, stood by me, answering—and asking—lots of questions, and allowed the vision of the book to unfold with her tremendous understanding and patience.

Special thanks go to my daughter Emily Davey for sticking by me through the project, editing and fine-tuning the manuscript, and being a happy kid when her mom was wondering if the book would ever be finished. You are terrific!

I'll always carry special memories of my grandma, Eleine Dunning, who took the time to teach me to knit and to make my own clothes, and of my mom, Elaine Eskesen, who taught me how to stand on my own two feet and how to create an attainable vision by allowing my passion to be expressed. You are always with me.

Special thanks also go to my Uncle George, who kept my spirits high, and to my sister, Sage, for being part of the scene and for helping in so many ways. Finally, to the rest of my wonderful family and friends—I thank you.

My family of knitters

1

the *magic* of
Color

why dye your own yarn?

*Color is life—life is color,
the vibrating, vitalic,
vitaminic energy manifest
in all animal, mineral and
vegetable nature.*

—Jacob Bonggren, quoted in
Healing and Regeneration Through Color
by Corinne Heline

Hand-dyed yarns bring colors into your life and can jazz up your next project.

An exciting part of my life as a yarn store owner is selecting the colors I want represented in my shop. This happens in two ways. First, yarn company representatives come twice a year to show me the new colors and yarns for the next season. From their selections, I pick out some unusual colors that add jazz to a project and I pick out some of the colors customers feel safe with. Then, I go into my studio and dye my own yarns.

I have noticed over the years that my palette is saturated with the colors I see every day. I love the earth tones of the tidal pools and the bright reds of the poppies in my garden. These colors speak to me—as they can speak to you, the knitter. Customers who come into my shop are drawn to the colors that surround them. They want to know where these vibrant fibers come from. When I say I dye them, they're amazed. When I tell them that they, too, can learn to dye yarns in colors of their own choosing, they are downright skeptical. Yet any knitter can learn to dye. If you have the desire to create colors that please you, and if you want to add your own personal touch to a project, then you, too, can dye your own yarns.

But *why* dye your own yarn? You might want particular shades for a favorite Fair Isle pattern, but even after traveling miles to visit numerous yarn stores, you can't find the range of colors in the correct weight of yarn for your envisioned project. You can shop on the Internet, but how can you know the colors are accurately represented on a Web site?

Color is all around us and is an important part of our daily life. Color can set a mood. Knitting a sweater for your first grandchild or a scarf for a trusted friend requires time, and the yarn is essential to the success of your labors. Finding the exact yarn desired for a specific project is sometimes difficult. The choices or range of colors may be limited, so we often improvise (or compromise). Now there is another choice: let the artist side of you take over and dye your own yarn. The good news is that it is not difficult to get satisfying colors in a variety of fibers that will yield pleasing results in a knitting project.

Make visible what, without you, might perhaps never have been seen.

—Robert Bresson

Friends Sherry and Pam and I find some time to knit together, leaving sleeping dog to lie.

We all have stashes of yarn, don't we? Many knitters have confessed to me that they have more yarn than they will ever be able to knit, yet they buy more. A color or texture speaks to them, and they want it for some unknown future project, so it goes into the stash. This is all well and good—we love our yarns. Yet, from a practical point of view, is this the most logical approach? The color we couldn't live without is now an eyesore with no future. Whether you are a knitter who plans every project or one who just picks out a yarn and knits, dyeing your own yarn gives you many options. It is more economical to work with a few dyes and some yarn, and you will find out shortly that you can always have the right color and texture.

Space-dyed wool colors dance around the circumference of a hat.

I find that knitters today engage in a more interactive role in the production of a project. In the past, most of us would pick out yarn that was shown as a sweater in the yarn store, with a pattern available. Or we'd use a pattern from a magazine, with a specific yarn to be used. Yarn companies made patterns to promote a certain yarn to the consumer, and our only choice was to select the color. The yarn companies would offer new choices in patterns and colors every year, yet the basic idea was still the same: knit what you see. The patterns and yarns were tried-and-true and consistent year after year.

That way of knitting is now being augmented with a more creative approach. Today's knitters love the feel of the fiber running through their fingers. They are curious, devoted to their craft, and can be adventurous and outrageous. The entire process—making something from start to finish—is exciting and interesting. This new era of knitting brings a new sense of the verb "to knit." Knitting is a creative outlet, and learning to dye your own yarns is another way to engage in this art form.

■ A PERSONAL APPROACH

Color is always around us. Making time to take a walk and look closely at something allows the childlike sense of wonder to reappear in our lives. Magic happens. How many different greens appear in a field of wildflowers or a grove of pines? Notice the subtleness of these soft differences and wonder how there can be so many colors. When I pay attention to these differences, I do not judge or say I don't like a color, I simply become aware of my natural surroundings.

I have developed a sense of color based directly on the world around me. I have no formal training in color theory or in putting colors together. Over the past twenty years I have become excited about color. I have taken the time to look closely and to focus on small details. Looking at color is very personal: it delights me, it intrigues me, and it allows a constant sense of love in my life. Looking at color requires solitude and quiet reflection so that I may find a way to work with it in the knitting world. By closely examining the colors in an autumn leaf, I am struck by the number of oranges, reds, and golds that can surface in one small spot, and the way the colors move into one another and into the texture of the leaf. This fascinates me. How do these colors affect what I am designing?

We all have the ability to see color, texture, and pattern. This book will help you with the process. As knitters, we already create things of beauty using our hands, two needles, and some yarn. Now it is time to allow the creative flow of color within each of us to be acknowledged and to blossom. Are you ready to join me in that exploration?

Each of us sees color from our own personal history. Once you start to look at colors, notice them in the fabric of your curtains, your wardrobe, fashion magazines, your children's or grandchildren's artwork, the paintings hanging on your walls, and the colors of your rooms. Notice how you react to some. Does a red velvet sofa feel cozy? Do you feel safe surrounded by a blue wall? Is there a lot of one color dominating your wardrobe? Are the walls in your house in the same color family?

What colors excite you? What colors bring back memories? When I was a student teacher in college, my advisor said, "Don't wear red in the classroom; it excites the students. Wear blue to keep the students quiet." I will never forget this statement. As I've studied more about color, I've realized she was right. I wear a lot of red, and I love excitement.

Think about how you react to certain colors. You probably already know what colors you are drawn toward—the ones you reach for on the shelf when you shop for yarn or clothes. Now take a journey inward. Spend some time alone with the colors you see on your walks and in your house and neighborhood. If you are lucky enough to have a stash of yarns, look through it and pick out some colors. Without thinking too much about it, use all the colors to knit a square of stockinette stitch. Play with the colors and experiment. When your swatch is done, what does it remind you of?

I find that knitters sometimes panic about putting more than one color into a project. To gain confidence, take the step to look at color combinations around you and put them to work in your own creations. The mystery of how to put colors together will be unlocked the minute you take a moment to focus. I don't think it is necessary to figure out *why* you like the combinations of colors you like, but do observe and take notes. Bring a sketch pad or camera with you so you can use this information later. Being creative requires solitude and a quiet place to work. Find some time, even ten minutes a day, to explore your own relationship with the colorful world that surrounds you. Trust me, it will be reflected in your knitting.

Lots of color will liven up simple seed stitch and stockinette patterns.

■ INSPIRATION FROM NATURE

When I lived on the Greek island of Paros for a year, I was given the chance to discover nature at its best. I spent hours in the countryside picking wildflowers, finding shells and interesting rocks by the sea, and sitting contentedly, watching darting lizards. My life became totally saturated with color: the turquoise sea, the famous Greek light, and the poppy fields at sunset. How I saw color changed. What happened? I was no longer distracted in my day-to-day life. My routine changed, and I took the time to notice things I had never before bothered to see. When I picked out tomatoes at the green grocer, I could smell their redness and ripeness. On the island, it was the little things that became important, and I delighted in my surroundings.

My first and earliest designs were done while I was living on Paros, and these early designs reflected my newly made discovery that nature supplies many opportunities for design. Walking hour after hour on narrow cobblestone streets, I watched the colors at different times of the day as the light changed from a brilliant white to a soft orange, providing many shadows and shades of one reflected color. I saw the sun appearing from behind the clouds, the early morning rain-swept stones, the earth and rocks warmed by the heavy dose of sunlight. These wondrous phenomena provided an appearance and mood that seemed supernatural. I noticed the incredible color combinations provided by nature, such as those in an individual flower or in the composition of hundreds of wildflowers in the fields of rock and olive groves. I noticed the moods that color creates and

Vibrant colors work together in a pattern inspired by the wildflowers on a Greek island.

how colors go together. I also started to look at the patterns in nature: the spiral on the snail's shell; the rough, twisted contortions of the olive tree; and how the sea and coves of the island had a rhythm of beauty. Observing was the beginning, and I also developed a sense of well-being as I recognized the beauty that surrounded me.

It was there on that small island that, out of necessity, I learned to dye wool. The roughly spun wool of the island sheep was white, and buying yarn in Athens meant a 16-hour boat ride in often rough winter seas. So I had an incentive to dye my own yarn if I wanted to create colorful patterns. Colored pencils and graph paper provided me with the tools I needed to start putting ideas and designs from my surroundings onto paper for a knitted garment.

Back on my farm in Maine, I began in earnest to dye wool in my summer kitchen. I continued to be absorbed in the many colorful facets that nature provided, and my dyed yarns were the result of my daily walks. I focused on little things: the iridescent green on dragonfly wings or the color of sap on a pine tree. I learned, and so can you.

Give some attention and focus, and your eyes will notice colors. Take a walk, even if it is just to your own backyard or down a busy city street. Instead of saying, "I have no interest in that," say, "I haven't yet become interested in that." Once you realize that the interest resides in your own being and not in the object itself, you will delight in a new life of seeing. Find ways to see beauty in nature. If a walk in the woods is impossible, a simple flower can inspire. Look at an iris and see the complexities of colors in that single flower. How many different shades of violet are there? The iris might be found in your garden, in a garden magazine, in a floral design on a fabric, or in a painting by van Gogh. Look at how the yellow pops out, surrounded by all that purple; its splash excites and stands out. The wonderful sense of color is also revealed in books such as Andy Goldsworthy's *A Collaboration with Nature*. So treat yourself to a new sense of wonder—open your eyes, become that child you once were, and begin again to see life's little creations.

■ APPLYING YOUR OWN SENSE OF COLOR

Once you have opened your eyes to the world of color around you and are ready for your knitting projects to reflect your own sense of color, it's time to fulfill your colorful visions by learning to dye yarn.

Natural textiles used for weaving, basketmaking, knitting, and other forms of expressive art are classified as either protein or cellulose fibers, based on their molecular structure and chemical composition. Protein fibers (such as wool and mohair) are based on animal hair, while cellulose fibers (such as cotton, rayon, and linen) come from plants. (Silk is also a protein fiber.) Dye is a substance used to color something using either a cold- or hot-water process. Specific types of dyes and dyeing procedures must be used for each type of fiber. The way the dye bonds with the fiber and the choice of dyeing assistant, or mordant, used to facilitate the process depend on the fiber being dyed. Usually, dyes that work well with protein fibers will not work with cellulose fibers, and vice versa.

An iris painted by my daughter Robin provides a wonderful statement about the bold color juxtapositions in nature.

Protein fibers are made up of amino acids, each type of fiber having its own composition and structure. Protein fibers vary in luster, resilience, and affinity for dyes, yet there is some consistency as to how dyes react with all the protein fibers.

In this book, I focus only on dyeing protein fibers using acid dyes. (A discussion of cellulose fibers and their dyeing techniques could fill another whole book.) Wool, mohair, silk, angora, and the other protein fibers make knitting yarns of unsurpassed beauty and versatility, and they take dye well. It is my hope that you will find hours of enjoyment and a great sense of fulfillment in discovering color and dyeing yarn for your own knitting projects.

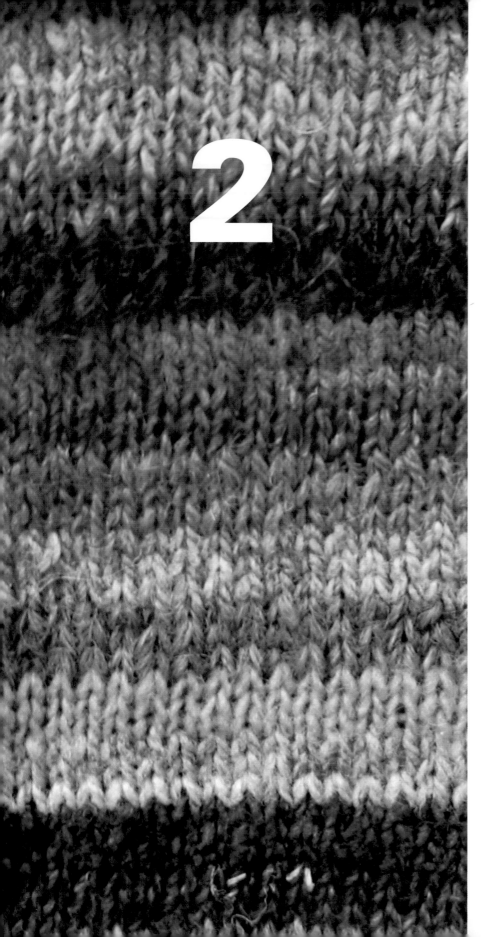

2

understanding color & color *relationships*

Color begins with light. In 1666 Sir Isaac Newton discovered the color spectrum when he observed that sunlight could be broken down into seven bands of color: red, orange, yellow, green, blue, indigo, and violet. Our perception of color is filtered by many layers of influence and interpretation: cultural, psychological, personal, artistic, physical, and scientific.

Dyeing yarn is all about color, and it is important to understand color theory and how to achieve the colors you want by using the color wheel. One art teacher used to tell us that putting colors together is intuitive—that it could not be taught. I certainly do not believe this. Most artists have a good understanding of how to put colors together, and choosing certain colors is no accident, but you do not have to be an artist to work with color. Color sense is innate in all of us, but it sometimes needs to be discovered. The best way to learn about this fascinating topic is to do it. Getting a feel for how to put colors together requires learning some of the fundamental principles and trying them out. A fun way to do this would be to invite a small group of knitters together to explore color and see how these theories work.

■ THE ALL-IMPORTANT COLOR WHEEL

Working with an artist's color wheel is one way to begin to understand color and color mixing, whether on an artist's palette, in a dye formula, or in the design of a knitted garment. I strongly recommend that you pick up this graphics tool, which can be purchased at any well-stocked art shop. Using the color wheel as a guide to where colors fit in the spectrum is an important education for the potential dyer.

Sunlight is composed of all colors, and the sequence—the color spectrum created when white light is refracted through a prism—is represented in the color wheel. Twelve hues—red, blue, yellow, orange, violet, green, red-orange, yellow-orange, yellow-green, blue-green, blue-violet, and red-violet—are the basis of the wheel. As you scan from one color toward the next on the wheel, you'll notice how the colors share the characteristics of their neighboring colors. The range of colors that can be mixed is infinite.

Hue, Saturation, and Value

Every color has three qualities: hue, saturation, and value.

HUE is the basic name of a color. In a twelve-hue color wheel there are three *primary* hues, three

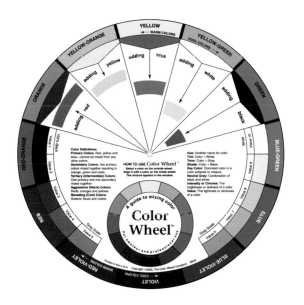

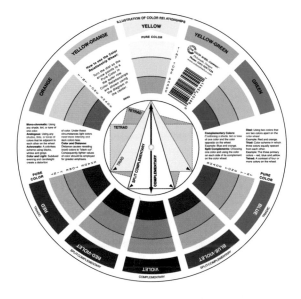

An artist's color wheel, front and back.

COURTESY OF
THE COLOR WHEEL CO.

secondary hues, and six *tertiary* (or *intermediate*) hues. A primary color is one that cannot be made from other colors. Mixing the primaries yields all the other colors. The primary colors are red, blue, and yellow, and the primary division of the color wheel is in thirds. Each primary color has some effect throughout the color wheel and directly affects the colors nearby.

Mixing equal amounts of two primary colors produces a secondary color. Red and yellow make orange, red and blue make violet (purple), and blue and yellow make green. The secondary colors add three more hues to the color wheel, so now we're up to six.

Mixing a primary and the adjacent secondary color makes a tertiary, or intermediate, color. Tertiary colors have compound names. A primary red and a secondary orange produce red-orange, for example. The other tertiaries are yellow-orange, yellow-green, blue-green, blue-violet, and red-violet. With the addition of the six tertiaries, the color wheel has a total of twelve hues.

SATURATION is the intensity of a color. Pure hues are the brightest, most vivid, and jewel-like. Duller colors can be made by mixing in a complementary color—such as adding green to red. You can also add black to a bright color. Neutral earth tones are a good example of lower intensity colors. Mixing two highly intense colors creates a mixed-dye color that is lower in intensity than either of the original colors.

VALUE, in color, is the range from dark to light. For a painter, it is how much gray a hue has when varying amounts of black are added. Raspberry is a light value of red, while maroon is a dark value. A tint moves toward white; pink is a light tint of red. A shade moves toward black; cranberry is a dark tint of red. A tone is modified with gray. Garnet is a tone of red. (Obviously, there is no white dye. You will need to use less dye to yield a paler color, whereas an artist can mix in white pigment to create a lighter tint. To get a darker value, use more dye.)

Looking at the color wheel, you'll see that yellow is the lightest color, going toward white, while violet is the darkest color, going toward black. Yellow and orange begin to lose their color identity as more black is added, but blue and violet just tend to show the color as a deeper shade.

Temperature of Color

Color can be viewed in many different ways. One way is according to *temperature*—reds and oranges are seen as the warmest colors, while violets, blues, and greens are seen as the coolest. We notice warm colors more than cool ones, which tend to recede and are passive in a design. The reds and oranges are often visualized as the warmth of a fire or the glow of a sunset. The greens and blues can represent the cool of the depths of the ocean or the leaves in a forest glen. When using colors, think about what makes a color warm or cool. A blue-green can look warmer in one context than in another, depending on its neighboring color. Each color has a temperature variation depending on its depth of shade, intensity, and value.

Again using the color wheel as a guide, find in your stash twelve yarns that resemble the hues on the wheel. Place them in a circle arranged by color temperature. Traditionally the cooler colors go from violet to yellow green; the warmer colors go from red-violet to yellow. Warm colors have more yellow and red and less blue. The cool colors have more blue and less red and yellow.

■ HARMONIES AND CONTRASTS

Michel Chevreul (1786–1889), the director of the dye house at the Gobelins tapestry mill, in Paris, wrote about color in *The Principles of Harmony and Contrasts of Colors*. In this book, he discussed simultaneous and successive contrast and five

Pines by the sea inspired this pleasing swatch of cool colors.

Gazing into a fire helped me pick out the warm colors found here.

principles of color harmony, all of which are useful concepts to keep in mind as you explore the possibilities of color in your knitting.

Simultaneous Contrast

When you view a bright color, your eye will automatically see the color's complement simultaneously. If you view a color for a few minutes and then look away to a neutral background, you will see the opposite color as an afterimage. For example, after looking at violet, the afterimage would be yellow. These opposite colors can look intense when used in bold areas of patterning, such as squares, and will have a striking visual effect. However, if these same colors are used in small stripes or lines, the eye will not be able to differentiate the colors. They will cancel each other out, and the overall effect will be dull. Opposite colors work well when juxtaposed in big areas of pattern and background; diffused, as in narrow stripes, the colors blend into mud.

We notice differences more than similarities in color. Dark colors will accent the brightness of adjacent lighter colors. Next to a bright, intense color, a dark color looks duller. The same neutral color will look dark against a lighter background and light against a darker background.

The Harmony of Adjacent Colors

Adjacent, or analogous, colors are pleasing in combination and therefore harmonious. These are the colors that are next to one another on the color wheel. Examples of adjacent colors are a primary color with both of its flanking tertiary colors, such

Adjacent colors on the color wheel, combined with inspiration from an iris blossom and its foliage, provided this colorway.

as yellow with yellow-orange and yellow-green. These colorful statements often show up in the glorious array of nature's color schemes: a sunset has a hint of violet next to the reds and oranges. Color combinations with three or four adjacent colors can produce a bold statement that can have an emotional effect simply by the selection of warm or cool colors.

The Harmony of Opposites

Here is where the old saying "opposites attract" can be clearly visualized. The contrast of opposite, or complementary, colors on the color wheel is well balanced and creates a feast for the eye. They energize one other and create a pleasant mixture of cool and warm. Complementary colors tend to bounce off and enliven a design or pattern. They also are most likely seen as pairs in nature. Look closely at a thistle and see the violet flower and the yellow stamen. Enjoy a field of poppies and see the intense red set off by the cool green. Note that the complement of a primary color is always a secondary color: red and green, blue and orange, yellow and violet.

Complementary colors heighten the intensity of one other when used in similar saturation levels, but not when one color is less saturated than the other; light blue and deep orange will not make the same color statement as deep blue with deep orange.

You can also make a dramatic statement by using combinations such as red and yellow-green or red and blue-green. Combinations of primary and secondary colors are more standard, but I personally

The tertiary colors yellow-green, red-orange, and yellow-orange, paired with their opposites of red-violet, blue-green, and blue-violet, present a beautiful balance of color.

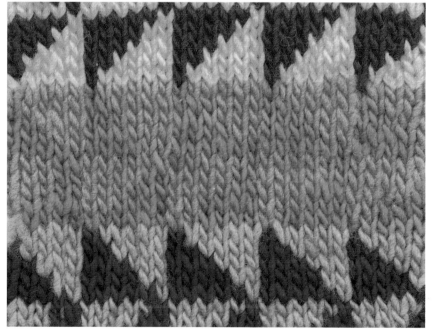

The primary colors yellow, blue, and red paired with their color-wheel opposites of violet, orange, and green create a balance of warm and cool colors.

like the more surprising effects of the tertiary colors. I love to observe the exciting combination of tertiary colors—red-violet and yellow-green are favorites of mine that show up constantly in our natural surroundings: the purplish blue mussel shell lying near rust-orange lichen on the rocks by the shore. The eye seems to like color combinations that reflect a strong opposition of hue, and any such pairing can make a striking statement.

Split Complements

We add another dimension to our color combinations by adding one more color. Split complementary color schemes comprise three colors—a hue with the two colors *adjacent to its opposite color* on the wheel. Take the color blue-violet and combine it with orange and yellow to make a striking split complement. These color combinations add a new heightened dimension to color combinations, yet stay within the system of the color wheel.

The Harmony of Triads

The color wheel can be dissected into four triads, all of which are exciting color combinations:

1. The primary colors of red, blue, and yellow
2. The secondary colors of violet, green, and orange
3. The tertiary colors of yellow-green, red-orange, and blue-violet
4. The tertiary colors of red-violet, yellow-orange, and blue-green

Use any of these combinations in a design, and it will be stunning. The primaries are the least sophisticated. They are frequently used in children's patterns and have a charm and happy appeal as a palette. The secondary colors remind me of nature's palette, and these can create interest as color combinations in Fair Isle and other patterns. The two tertiary color triads cause a sensation

An example of a split complement using the blue-violet hue and the yellow and orange to make one color statement. Also try yellow-green with red and violet.

when used in knitted designs, and add an impulsive, creative whimsy to a project, making it fun to design. When stepping around the color wheel, take an opportunity to visit these triads and decide for yourself which ones are exciting and challenging to work with.

The Harmony of a Dominant Tint

Usually your color combination will have a dominant color. It can suggest a theme, such as those seen in natural surroundings: the blues in the night sky, the greens of trees in a forest, or the balance of oranges during a sunset. The dominant tint brings a group of colors together by providing a central unifying—and usually understated—tone. It adds balance to a design.

Space-dyed yarns in the secondary colors of orange and violet, with a splash of tertiary yellow-green, make a colorful swatch using a textured stitch.

A dominant color will bring colors together to suggest a theme such as an evening sunset, with dominant red

3

Dyeing Procedures

The inspired artist and the practical craftsperson come together when a knitter decides to dye his or her own yarn. As an artist, I see color in a new way every day—one day my eye might notice a golden lichen color, the next day a moss green. Many of the colors you see may not be available in yarns, so, unless you dye your own, your palette is limited to the colors supplied by yarn companies. Color is so exciting, but finding a color you like somewhere and not being able to match it in a yarn store can be frustrating.

In this chapter I will give you the information to change all that: a primer on dyeing protein fibers, a discussion of some of the unique qualities of different protein fibers, the basics of how to safely set up a dye studio, and the details of the dyeing process. I also will introduce some of my tried-and-true dye techniques and talk about experimental yarn dyeing.

■ A PRIMER ON USING WASHFAST ACID DYES

A dye is a substance used to color something using a cold- or hot-water process. Specific dyes and dyeing techniques are used with certain fibers. This book focuses on dyeing protein (animal-based) fibers with acid dyes. (Interestingly enough, nylon has a similar molecular structure and also works well with this type of dye.)

For these dyes to react to fiber, several things must be present: acid, heat, and time. In a dye bath, water, dye, fiber, and acid all work together to allow the dye molecules to bond with the fiber. Acid dyes can be applied to natural protein fibers, such as wool and silk, to create beautiful hand-dyed yarns.

The acid is the dye assistant, or mordant. Acids can range from strong (sulfuric acid) to weak (citric acid). Weak acid dyes are recommended for the craftsperson working in a home studio. They are easy to use, clean up well, and can be stored as a stock solution for future projects. Which weak acid you choose, and the amount used, are both important. Several acids are available to the home dyer. White vinegar, readily available, is approximately a 5 percent solution of acetic acid, but it can get expensive if you are dyeing large amounts of fiber. Dilute acetic acid can be bought in bulk from a dye company, but it has a strong odor, and if you are using it in an enclosed area, the smell can be overwhelming. The third choice of weak acid is citric acid, in granular form, which can be easily measured and added to a dye solution. Citric acid, which is also used to preserve fruit when making jam, has no objectionable odor and is easily stored. Best of all, you don't need

Nature provides a beautiful array of colors in this fascinating tide pool.

very much of it. I have used citric acid for many years because of these desirable factors. For economic and safety reasons, citric acid is the best choice.

For this book, I have chosen to work with WashFast acid dyes, classified in the weak category, because they are relatively safe to use and reliable in dyeing protein fibers. They are easy to control when mixing and when heating in the dye bath, and they come in an incredible range of colors. WashFast acid dyes test well for both washfastness (ability to keep color when washed) and lightfastness (ability to keep color when exposed to sunlight). Used properly, they will produce beautiful results with a minimum of preparation or expense. They are manufactured by PRO Chemical and Dye, which offers 29 colors and several acid assistants (see Suppliers, page 126). For people who are just getting started in dyeing, I have put together a sampler kit of the primary colors plus violet and black, citric acid, Synthrapol, and a pocket-size artists' color wheel (order from www.pinetreeyarns.com).

Acid and dye are added together to the dye pot at the beginning of the process. The amount of acid in the dye bath is important. If there is not enough, the dye might not completely affix to the fiber. In that case, dye will remain in the dye bath and the bath will appear colored (instead of clear, as it should be) after the yarn is removed. If this happens, you can add more acid to the dye bath, resubmerge the yarn, and the remaining dye will affix to the fiber.

Heat is needed for the chemical reaction to occur between fiber and dyes, but it must be increased gradually. The dye reaction starts slowly, but as the temperature rises to around 160°F (71°C), bonding occurs rapidly, until all the dye has been exhausted and the dye bath becomes clear. It is important to stir the fiber slowly during heating so the dye will be distributed evenly.

Time is also an important part of the dyeing process. It takes time to bring the temperature up to the point that the chemical reaction can occur. After the dye has been affixed to the fiber, the temperature must remain constant (just below boiling) to ensure washfastness and lightfastness. The dye bath must run the recommended time—in this case one hour—to achieve the desired results. After an hour, turn the heat off and allow the fiber to cool in the dye bath before you rinse or handle it.

■ WORKING WITH NATURAL FIBERS

Natural protein fibers—such as wool and silk—are readily available in most yarn shops. They take dye happily and are relatively inexpensive. The market is expanding to include useful blends of wool and silk, in which two fibers are combined to make a yarn softer than pure wool yet more elastic than pure silk. Many blends such as wool and mohair, wool and silk, mohair and nylon, and alpaca and wool can be easily dyed. We are now also being introduced to such exotic fibers as qiviut, the undercoat of the musk ox. Blending these exotics with wool makes them affordable and versatile. Cashmere blends, angora blends, and llama blends are all found in natural white or shades of gray and light brown, which can be dyed beautifully. Each fiber takes the dye differently and at different rates, yielding a range of yarn colors from the same dye pot, depending on the fiber. Every type of fiber has a place in some project, so it is fun to experiment with them in the dye pot.

Natural fibers of silk, silk noil, mohair, and wool are the bare canvas that awaits the artist-dyer's palette of color.

Wool

Produced by many different breeds of sheep, wool offers versatile qualities for the knitter and dyer. For novice dyers, it is best to start with wool; you can get good results, and the raw material is inexpensive. Wool has many positive attributes, including resilience, ease of wear, warmth, and wrinkle resistance. It blends well with other fibers, such as silk or llama, and its elasticity helps keep the fabric soft and flexible.

Wool is graded according to the diameter and length of its fiber. Fine wools are soft, elastic, warm, and the least abrasive next to your skin. Medium and heavy wool can be coarse and itchy, yet warm, and are best used for outer garments and rugs.

Wool can shrink and felt (i.e., the fibers permanently matt together) if not handled correctly in the dye pot. The same scaly outer layer that causes felting also makes wool initially resistant to water and dyes; however, the dyes bond easily with the fibers once the wool has been heated. Wool can be heated all the way to a boil (212°F; 100°C), but the heating must be gradual and the fibers must be stirred slowly and gently in the dye bath.

Silk

Silk fibers come from the secretions of a caterpillar as it spins its cocoon. The cocoon is spun from one continuous filament of silk, sometimes reaching 900 meters long. To harvest silk fibers, cocoons are gathered and heated in boiling water to dissolve the glue that keeps the filament together.

Bombyx mori is the most common silkworm used in the industry. It produces a white silk. Another silk that is often used is tussah. It is the color of honey because the leaves the silkworms eat contain tannin. Both *Bombyx* and tussah silks are strong, warmer than wool by weight, and more resistant to pilling and felting.

Silk is wonderful to dye, and its resulting colors are clear and lustrous. It dyes more quickly than wool, and it is able to react with the dye molecule at a lower temperature: 185°F (85°C). Dyeing silk at too high a temperature can damage the fiber, which then loses its luster and strength. In preparing silk for dyeing, I use hotter water than for wool (warm instead of lukewarm) and more of the wetting agent (Synthrapol) to allow the fiber to open up to be dyed. I find that silk takes more time to get wetted out, so I allow several hours, or leave it overnight, to get it thoroughly wet.

When wet, silk smells like rotting fish on the seashore, but it loses this odor when it dries. I also find that I often need to add a little more dye solution as the heating process continues because the dye does not always settle evenly on the fiber. Silk is weakest when it is wet, so be careful to keep the water temperature just below boiling and stir it gently. (Silk also has a tendency to get tangled, and sometimes wrinkled-looking, when wet. When rinsing and hanging it to dry, snap and pull the skein so it goes back to its original shape.)

In blends, silk adds strength, luster, and softness. I love dyeing silk, but for new dyers, I do not recommend space-dyeing or hand-painting it. With

SILK NOIL comes from the inner core of the cocoon and is the leftovers from the silk processing—the shorter fibers left after the silk is combed. It is strong and firm but does not have the luster of other silks, and, when it takes the dye, the color is muted, not bright.

these methods, the dye does not get fully absorbed into the skein, and you can end up with a muddy, blotchy appearance, without the intense colors so glorious on silk.

Mohair

Mohair—one of my favorite fibers to dye—is lustrous, strong, wrinkle-resistant, and adds more color to blends. It can add depth of color and texture to your project. Mohair comes from the Angora goat, which is sheared twice a year for its long, shiny hair. The finest mohair is from the first shearing of a kid goat. Mohair can be light and fuzzy or dense and thick. The fibers are not as elastic as wool, so if you aren't careful, they can get matted in the dye pot. Mohair does not shrink, but it can felt easily if given too hot a temperature and rough handling. It dyes beautifully and accepts the dye quickly. Keep the dye pot at a lower temperature (185°F; 85°C) than for wool, because the fiber needs less time to absorb the dye. Thicker-spun mohair needs more wetting out time than its lighter counterpart. Mohair can be space-dyed and hand-painted with decent results, but it is always easiest to start by observing how a fiber will react by immersion dyeing, with one solid color, in the dye pot.

Alpaca and Llama

Alpaca and llama fibers come from South American relatives of the camel. Both animals are native to the Andes Mountains. Alpaca and llama fibers are long and straight and not as elastic as wool. They are dense and heavy compared to wool, and very soft and warm. They take dye more lightly and have a softer look than wool or silk. Both fibers behave beautifully in a blend, adding softness to wool.

Angora

Angora rabbits produce a fur that is gathered by being plucked or brushed. Angora's main characteristic is its fluffiness, which gives loft to garments. Angora should be blended with wool or other fibers for several reasons. First, an all-angora garment will probably be too warm to wear, and all-angora yarn can be unstable because the fibers are so very fine and slippery. Also, angora should be blended to be successfully dyed. It takes dye differently from other fibers—dyeing lighter than wool—which adds subtle variations to dyed blended yarns.

Cashmere

Cashmere comes from the downy undercoat of the cashmere goat. The fibers are very soft and warm. It is very expensive because the goats produce only a small amount of fiber each year. It is wonderful in a blend and, as with angora, will take the dye differently from its blended counterpart.

Qiviut

Qiviut is the fiber from the downy undercoat of a musk ox. It is extremely expensive and hard to collect—usually being gathered tuft by tuft from underbrush as the animals shed. It blends beautifully with merino wool and other fibers, maintaining its softness and warmth.

■ SAFETY FIRST!

Safety is a primary concern for any dyer, and if you are using chemical dyes for the first time, please read this section carefully.

Dyeing beautiful yarn is fairly straightforward, but you *are* working with chemicals and boiling water, so you must be extremely cautious and use common sense. The WashFast acid dyes described in this book are considered relatively nontoxic, but they should be handled with appropriate care.

If possible, find a separate space in your studio or home to establish a dye area. You will need a stovetop or hotplate for these hot-water dyes. If you must dye in your kitchen, make sure no young children are present during the dyeing process. Also, put newspaper on the surfaces where you mix the dyes and thoroughly clean the area when you are done, wiping down all counter surfaces and the stovetop and sink area. Be neat, and if you spill something, clean it up immediately with paper towels, which can be easily discarded. Make sure all dyes and dye equipment are put away in a storage area where no one can get to them; do *not* keep them in the kitchen. All dyes should be labeled clearly so they cannot be mistaken for something else.

All dye equipment must be used *only* for dyeing. **DO NOT use your kitchen pots or any other cooking equipment for any dyeing project.** Buy a 20-gallon stainless steel pot for the sole purpose of dyeing yarn, or find some old pots that need a new home. You will also need measuring cups, plastic spoons, a set of measuring spoons, and a long-handled wooden spoon to stir the yarn.

Good ventilation is extremely important when you are dyeing yarn. Open a window near the stove. If possible, use an exhaust fan over the stovetop to pull the fumes outside once you start heating the dye bath. **However, do not turn on the exhaust fan until after the dye powder has been mixed into a liquid dye stock solution.** If you experience an adverse reaction to the fumes (such as lightheadedness or nausea), stop what you are doing and move away from the dyeing area to some fresh air—outside if possible. If you find that the symptoms persist as you dye more yarn, stop the project and consult with your doctor. If you have safety concerns, contact PRO Chemical and request a Materials Safety Data Sheet.

When working with the dry dye powder, use an approved dust mask, available from PRO Chemical or another dye company. Handling the powder is the most hazardous part of dyeing, as the particles are very fine and can easily be inhaled. Do not have a fan turned on nearby or a window open wide when you are measuring dyes, as the powders might fly around. Always put the lid securely on the dye jar when you are finished measuring, and never leave an open jar unattended.

If you dye a lot or have a big project in mind, buy a respirator, available through dye companies such as PRO Chemical. Use the respirator when space-dyeing to avoid inhaling dye fumes while yarn is simmering on the stove. The primary hazards for lung irritation are from the inhalation of dry dye particles or dye fumes when the dye is simmering.

Always wear rubber gloves, because chemicals from dye solutions or dry powder can be absorbed into the bloodstream through your skin. Spills can occur while you are adding water to the dye powder, so always have paper towels handy. It is a good idea to keep a set of clothes solely for dyeing and to wear protective clothing, such as an apron. Find a place to store these items in your studio so you can keep the dye process separate from the rest of your house.

Do not eat, drink, or smoke in the area while dyeing. It is not a good idea to dye if you are pregnant or nursing a baby. If you are dyeing in your kitchen, take a block of time to focus only on the dyeing process, so there is no conflict with cooking dinner or making cocoa for the kids. Do not allow children or pets in the kitchen or dye studio while you are working. Make sure the area is cleared of clutter on the floor so you do not trip on anything while carrying heavy pots full of water or dye.

Do not dye when you are tired or in a hurry. Dyes and mordants, like any chemicals, can be hazardous if used carelessly. Take the process seriously. Find a safety routine that works for you and stick with it so that little catastrophes don't happen.

SPECIAL NOTES ABOUT DISPOSAL: Dyes and chemicals used in small amounts by home dyers are not going to hurt the town sewer or your septic system if you pour them down the drain. Make sure the dye bath is exhausted, meaning it looks clear and colorless, before disposing of it. If you are concerned, add baking soda to the dye bath to neutralize the acidity prior to disposing of it.

■ SETTING UP A SUCCESSFUL, YET SIMPLE, DYE STUDIO

Ideally, you have a separate laundry area or basement with a sink and work space to use as a dye studio. However, this is not always possible. The space does not need to be particularly large, but it should have both good natural light and good overhead lighting. It is important to be able to see what you are doing, especially as beautiful colors are created. Natural daylight is always best; colors can shift significantly when viewed under fluorescent or incandescent light.

A nearby sink is very important, as water is a necessary ingredient to all aspects of the dyeing process. Water is also heavy, and carrying it from one location to another can be tiring.

A stove is needed as a heat source, so try to find an old 2- or 4-burner stove that will only be used for dyeing. Although it is an option, I do not recommend using a hot plate as it takes too long to heat the water, and I worry about the safety of extension cords or overloaded electrical outlets. Outside dyeing facilities can be set up for warm months or warm climates, using a gas grill, propane stove, or an outside fire pit.

A good work surface—counter space or a long table or old door—is also important for the dyer. You need room for the process of mixing dyes.

Wherever you set up your dye area, make sure you have a dedicated, secure storage space for your dyeing equipment and supplies where they will be out of reach of children and away from family traffic. Dye jars and stock solution bottles must be labeled.

The dye studio at my Pine Tree Yarns shop has plenty of work space and good natural light.

■ DYEING EQUIPMENT

As I mentioned above, all equipment bought for, or used in, the dye studio needs to be used solely for the purpose of dyeing yarns. Here is a list of basic equipment needed for the home dyer. Most items can be bought at a local hardware store or found in your home.

Dye Pots

This is often the most expensive purchase for the new dyer but also the most important. The pot needs to be large enough to hold the fiber and sufficient water to give good circulation yet be light enough to carry from sink to stove. I use a 20-gallon (75-liter) size for big dye jobs (a pound, or about 454 grams, of fiber) and a 10-gallon (38-liter) pot or big saucepan for smaller quantities.

Pots should be made of materials that will not affect the dye process by leaching metals into the water—aluminum or iron pots should not be used for this reason. Stainless steel is my preference. An enamel canning pot is fine as long as it has no cracks or chips that expose the iron beneath, as this will change the chemistry of the dye bath.

Items for Measuring & Mixing

- ■ SCALE for weighing dry fiber
- ■ PLASTIC OR GLASS MEASURING CUPS for liquid, with lips for easy pouring (I have six for mixing solutions)
- ■ STAINLESS STEEL MEASURING SPOONS for measuring the dye powders accurately
- ■ WOODEN SPOONS for stirring dye and fiber in the dye pot. The dye tends to stain the wood, but it does not contaminate the next dye pot. You may want several spoons for different colors, as I have. GLASS RODS can also be used to stir and lift the yarn while in the dye pot.
- ■ Disposable PLASTIC SPOONS for mixing the dye solutions

Your dyeing equipment must be dedicated to the sole purpose of dyeing fibers in the studio.

Protective Clothing

■ A HEAVY-DUTY APRON is essential—after all, you are working with dyes and hot water. Wearing old clothes—perhaps having one set of clothes to wear only for dyeing—is also helpful, as you will spill solutions from time to time. I have ruined some decent clothes over the years.

■ Good RUBBER GLOVES to protect your hands when handling the wetted fibers and rinsing your dyed wool

■ DISPOSABLE DUST MASKS are necessary while handling the dry dyes.

■ A RESPIRATOR to wear when you are simmering the fiber, to keep from breathing harmful fumes

Other Equipment

■ PLASTIC SQUEEZE BOTTLES to use for hand-painting yarns

■ CANDY THERMOMETER for checking water temperature

■ BOTTLES (glass or plastic) with good caps for storing mixed dyes (stock solutions)

■ WOODEN DOWEL for space-dyeing yarn

Items that Come in Handy

■ NEWSPAPERS, to put down when mixing dyes

■ PAPER TOWELS and SPONGE for clean up

■ POT HOLDERS to carry hot dye pots

■ Notebook or index cards for writing down formulas and taking notes

■ SCISSORS

■ PLASTIC TABLECLOTH

Heat Source

A 4-burner stove is best for this purpose; I love gas stoves, as it is easier to regulate their heat. You can use a 2-burner stove, or when dyeing outside, you can use a camp stove, a gas grill, or a fire pit.

Water and Water Source

Water is obviously an important ingredient, as the dyeing process uses large quantities of it. Water quality will be different for each household—a city dweller's water supply will have additives such as chlorine, while the well water at a rural house may have naturally occurring minerals. You may have a water softening system. These chemicals will affect the chemistry in the dye bath. This would be a problem only if for some reason you had to change location (and water source) partway through a big dyeing project that required absolutely consistent results.

It is best to have a stainless steel sink with both hot and cold water. It's also helpful to have a washing machine; I presoak all my yarn in the washing machine.

Dye Materials

■ WashFast acid dyes

■ Citric acid (mordant)

■ Synthrapol SP (wetting agent)

See Suppliers, page 126, or order as a kit from www.pinetreeyarns.com.

NOTE: Some dyeing instructions say to also add salt to the dye bath to ensure even, consistent color. I dye specifically to create beautiful variegated colors, so I do not use salt.

■ PREPARING YARN FOR DYEING

One of my sentiments about working with fiber is: love the yarn that you are knitting. Select fibers that you love and that fit the project you will be making. For ideas, look at the pattern section beginning on page 78. Also, remember that WashFast acid dyes will only dye protein (animal) fibers, not cellulose (plant) fibers.

The selection and preparation of the yarns will make or break any project. Wool is easy to dye and is the best fiber choice for your first projects.

Dye more yarn than is required for a project so you will have a surplus if you want to make your garment larger.

Making Skeins

If the yarn you have selected to dye is in a ball or on a cone, you must put it into a reeled skein before you dye it. To do this you can use a wooden or metal swift expanded to its widest circumference. If you do not have a swift, you can wind the yarn around your elbow and outstretched arm, holding it in your hand to secure it. If you are winding a large amount

Select yarns that intrigue you.

off a cone, keep the skeins at approximately 4 ounces (113g) for easier dyeing and handling. When you finish skeining, tie each yarn end loosely around the reeled skein. Using thick wool or cotton scrap yarn (do not use a dark color, or it might run when dyed), tie each skein in several places, evenly spaced, using a loose figure-eight loop or square knot. This will secure the yarn so that it will not get tangled while being dyed. Keep the ties loose—if they are too tight, the dye will not be able to penetrate beneath them and you will end up with an undyed (tie-dyed) area in your skein.

If you are space-dyeing yarn and want a consistent look in your project, make sure all your skeins are the same length. You can use different textures, but they need to be skeined up in the same manner so the color intervals will be consistent.

If yarns need to be weighed for a project, do the weighing before the skeins are wetted, and keep a record.

A swift

Wetting Out the Yarn

Once the yarn is skeined up, it must be "wetted out" prior to dyeing. This step is very important. Whether you are using handspun yarn, a commercial yarn, or yarn with lots of lanolin, you need to remove as much dirt and residue as possible to ensure even dyeing on the skein. I recommend using Synthrapol SP (a wetting agent) for this process. If Synthrapol SP is not available, a mild detergent such as Ivory Liquid can be used.

Fill a sink or washing machine with lukewarm water, adding a teaspoon of Synthrapol SP. Gather the skeins and put them in the sink. Wearing your rubber gloves, push the yarn under the water (air bubbles will surface) to get it consistently wetted out. If you are using the washing machine for wetting out, use the large load setting on the machine, add the wetting agent, agitate to mix it in, and then stop the wash cycle prior to adding the yarn. (Do not let the agitator kick in while your skeins are soaking!)

Soak the yarn for at least 30 minutes. Without lifting the skeins out of the water, inspect them to make sure they are thoroughly wet. Silk and silk blends should soak several hours or overnight because it takes a longer time for these fibers to absorb water. Any dry spots on the skein will not take the dye properly.

Be sure to handle wet fiber carefully. Do not agitate the skeins or lift them up while soaking. Let the fiber drain in the sink or use the spin cycle of your washing machine to spin out the excess water. Lift out the drained yarn, squeezing out excess water, and put it in a plastic bag or the dye pot until you are ready to proceed.

■ DYE MIXING AND PREPARATION

I love mixing dyes and watching to see how adding a few drops of one color can change the composition of a mixture. It is at this juncture of the process that you will begin to know your personal approach to dyeing. It is time to experiment, to begin to understand how to use the color wheel, and to decide what routines work for you.

Preparing Dye Stock Solutions

Making dye stock solutions is the first step whenever you are dyeing yarn. The dye powder must be dissolved in hot water to make a stock solution, which is what is added to the dye bath. The stock solutions can be mixed with each other to create as many colors as you like. The WashFast acid dye powders can be kept for years if stored at room temperature in a dry place. The dye stock solutions, stored in tightly capped glass or plastic bottles, may be kept for at least 6 months.

Make dye stock solutions by mixing 1 teaspoon of dye, 1 tablespoon of citric acid, and one cup of water. The solutions are then blended to make the specific colors you desire.

Remember to put on your rubber gloves and dust mask before you handle or mix the powdered dyes.

On a covered work surface, place five measuring cups and the jars of powdered dye you plan to use. (The dyes I selected for the sampler kit mentioned below are the primary colors plus violet and black.)

In each measuring cup, put 1 teaspoon (5ml) of dry dye, then add 2 tablespoons (15ml) of boiling water, and stir with a plastic spoon to make a paste. If you are using one set of measuring spoons, wipe the measuring spoon with a damp paper towel to remove any dye particles, before going on to the next color. Add 1 cup of warm water to each vessel, then thoroughly mix each solution with its own separate plastic spoon, so no contamination occurs. Add 1 tablespoon of citric acid to each cup. (I use citric acid instead of acetic acid, because it does not have a bad odor. The terrible smell of acetic acid is only made worse when confined to a small dyeing space.)

While making the dye stock solutions, you will notice several things. For example, each color has its own individual odor (but don't sniff too enthusiastically when confirming this observation!) Also, Violet 817 tends to glob when mixing, so mix it with extra care, and make sure the water is *hot*. Violet is a deep, saturated color, and it takes a long time to dissolve. I have a separate measuring cup just for violet.

Once you have completed this procedure using the dyes in the sampler kit, you'll have a stock solution for each primary color plus black and violet. You can see each color by looking at its plastic spoon or by holding the cup up to the light. The next step is to use the stock solutions to mix custom colors for your palette.

Experimenting with Color

So that I can see the dye colors, I like to mix my dye solutions in a glass jar or clear measuring cup, one that allows for easy pouring. If you don't have a large supply of these, you can use any clear vessels.

Once you start mixing dyes, you can rely on the color wheel for general guidance, but now is the time to experiment. I often take out my watercolors and play with the colors on paper before I mix them as dyes.

With an empty cup and the stock solutions in front of you, decide on a base color and pour some of that solution into the empty cup. Now add a second color a little at a time until you see a new color develop. STOP! Stir the blend with a new spoon and see what magic happens. Drop a small amount of your dye mixture on a white piece of paper or paper towel to see what the color looks like. The more dye you put in, the more intense the color will be. There is some guesswork involved here, and that is the fun part of learning to dye. As you work, you will begin to see and understand how colors are created. Practice will give you the confidence to find a way to mix your own palette. Experimenting with drops of color will give you knowledge of how dyes come together to make a new color.

If you have any left-over stock solutions, store them in individual jars with easy screw-on caps. Label each jar with the color name, using a permanent marker (this is important because the name might get smeared if you pick up the jar when wearing wet gloves).

Playing with watercolors and seeing how the colors work together on paper will help you decide what color combinations you want to use in your yarns.

■ PREPARING THE DYE BATH AND DYEING YARN

Using a stainless steel or enameled pot of adequate size to let the fiber move freely in the dye bath, add about 4 gallons of warm water to dye one pound of yarn. The rule of thumb is 30 or 40 parts of water to one part of fiber.

It's easiest to work this calculation using metric measures. For example, if you have a 100-gram skein of yarn: 40 times 100 is 4,000 grams, or 4 liters of water. (That's slightly over a gallon of water for 3.5 ounces of yarn, not 1 gallon for 4 ounces. Rule-of-thumb metric/English equivalents are rarely precise. This is one reason why it is important to keep detailed notes if you think you might ever want to exactly duplicate a particular color.)

For smaller quantities of yarn, you can use proportionately less water and a smaller dye pot—but make sure the pot is large enough that you can stir the yarn in the dye bath without spilling!

Pour in your prepared dye stock solution and stir thoroughly with a wooden spoon. Add the yarn slowly and gently stir it in the dye pot. Turn on the stove and allow the dye bath to gradually come to a simmer—212°F or 100°C for wool; 185°F or 85°C for silk, mohair, or cashmere—continuing to slowly stir the pot from time to time. Simmer the skeins for an hour, then turn off the stove and allow them to cool slowly in the dye bath. When they are completely cool, rinse them thoroughly with lukewarm water.

■ SPECIFIC DYEING TECHNIQUES

Now that you are familiar with the basic steps for mixing dye stock solutions and preparing and using the dye bath, I'll give specific instructions for several different dyeing procedures. First I will introduce three techniques that yield enormously different results: dyeing solid colors, space-dyeing, and hand-painting. With the first two, the dyed colors will be clear and strong because the skeins are immersed in the dye pot. On hand-painted yarns, the colors will be more subtle and blended, as we are working on the surface of the fiber and using a smaller amount of dye.

Then I will go on to describe how to dye different types of fibers together, followed by a discussion of overdyeing. Last, I will talk about several experimental dyeing techniques.

Dyeing solid colors using various fibers will set the stage for many future knitting projects.

■ DYEING SOLID COLORS

When I started to hand-paint and dye my own wool, I would devise color formulas and write them on index cards. As my fascination grew and my creative palette took on a life of its own, I stopped writing down formulas because I eventually discovered that I could rely on my instincts to come up with wonderful colors. Sometimes this seems a little like cooking; I'll use "a dab" of a particular dye, not a precise amount. But for someone just learning the techniques, precise directions are reassuring. For you, the new dyer, whether adventurous or intimidated, I will first give tips on how to get the perfect intensity of color in your project, followed by some of my favorite color formulas.

equipment

- 20-gallon (75-liter) stainless steel or enameled pot
- Measuring cups
- Set of measuring spoons
- Plastic spoons
- Wooden stirring spoon
- Color wheel
- Dust mask
- Rubber gloves

materials

- One pound (454g) of yarn
- Sampler kit of WashFast acid dyes, which includes Synthrapol SP and citric acid (available from www.pinetreeyarns.com)

If the yarn you are using is in pull-skeins or on cones, make it into reeled skeins and wet it out, as described on pages 31–32.

Let's start with one-color value graduations or depth of shade, going from pale to deep. The following formulas are for dyeing one pound of fiber. If you want to dye only half a pound (two 4 oz skeins), halve the amount of dye in the dye bath. To dye one 4 oz skein, use one-quarter the amount of dye.

Please remember to handle dyes safely; put on your gloves and dust mask before proceeding.

To experiment with dyeing a particular shade of one color, choose a color from the sampler kit: Black, Violet 817, Red 349, Blue 490, or Yellow 119.

The formulas for depth of shade are listed below. To use these formulas, you need to weigh the yarn before you start, because the amount of dye powder needed to achieve a particular shade is determined by the weight of the fiber, as noted above.

AMOUNT OF DYE POWDER NEEDED TO DYE ONE POUND (454g) OF YARN

Shade	Dye Powder
Pale	½ teaspoon (1.2g)
Light/medium	1 teaspoon (2.5g)
Medium/dark	2 teaspoons (5g)
Dark	3 teaspoons (7.5g)
Intense dark	4 teaspoons (10g)

Mix according to the directions given on pages 32–33 for preparing the dye stock solution. Please note that when measuring, the teaspoon must be kept level to achieve consistent results. Also, a very small amount of "stray" dye can change the color you are trying to make.

Depth of shade can be determined by how much dye you use for a certain amount of fiber. The more dye, the more intense a shade. Less dye will achieve a pale shade.

6 intermediate colors of the color wheel. (You might wish to use Violet 817 from the dye sampler kit rather than mixing your own violet.)

There are 12 segments of the color wheel; to be consistent, we will use 12 tablespoons of prepared dye stock solution and one ounce (28.5 grams) of fiber for each color on the wheel (12 ounces or 340 grams of fiber, total).

Colors made with these formulas are quite saturated. You can make a slightly less intense color wheel by using 10 tablespoons per color rather than 12. I chose the 12-tablespoons formula to make the proportions into equal ratios. You can also choose to change the proportions slightly if you like. For instance, add a little more blue dye or a little less red dye to make a bluer blue-violet.

Use the same amount of citric acid for your dye stock solution regardless of how pale or deep the finished color will be: one tablespoon for each pound of fiber (25g of crystals per 454g of fiber).

Follow the dyeing directions on page 34 for dyeing your solid-color skein(s). Once you are familiar with how to create the shades you desire using one or more of the off-the-shelf WashFast acid dye colors, you can proceed to the next adventures: color mixing and making your own custom colors.

Color Mixing Using the Color Wheel

Hue graduation is a method for mixing colors, using the color wheel to generate some basic formulas—these give you a starting point for your own formulas. First, make a stock solution for each primary color. You will use these to mix the 3 secondary and

---

TIP: Dye molecules for each color are different; dyes have different mixing ratios.

Remember that this is only a starting-out point for you as a dyer. **As you mix, adjust the dye stock solutions to suit your taste. It is important to note that the yarn will look darker when it is wet and in the dye bath.**

Mixing colors is all about proportions. A lighter color (such as yellow) will need more dye if you are putting it with a darker color (such as blue) to make a spring green. Being consistent is the difficult part, but who wants to be consistent? Unless you are a professional dyer, and need exact formulas to be reproduced, you can mix anything. When the color is right, you'll know it.

To Dye	Use This Much Dye Stock Solution
Primary yellow	12 Tbsp (177.5ml) Yellow
Yellow-orange	11 Tbsp (163ml) Yellow, ¼ tsp (1.25ml) Red
Orange	6 Tbsp (88.75ml) Red; 6 Tbsp (88.75ml) Yellow
Red-orange	9 Tbsp. Red (133ml); 3 Tbsp (44.25ml) Yellow
Red	12 Tbsp (177.5ml) Red
Red-violet	9 Tbsp (133ml) Red; 3 Tbsp (44.25ml) Blue
Violet	6 Tbsp (89ml) Red; 6 Tbsp (89ml) Blue
	or 12 Tbsp (177.5ml) Violet 817
Blue-violet	3 Tbsp (44.25ml) Red; 9 Tbsp (133ml) Blue
Blue	12 Tbsp (177.5ml) Blue
Blue-green	9 Tbsp (133ml) Blue; 3 Tbsp (44.25ml)Yellow
Green	6 Tbsp (88.75ml) Blue; 6 Tbsp (88.75ml) Yellow
Yellow green	11¾ (174ml) Tbsp. Yellow; ¼ tsp (1.25ml) Blue

Tbsp = tablespoon   tsp = teaspoon

A 12-hue color wheel of skeins is achieved by mixing 3 primary colors in a specific ratio for each of the 12 colors to be dyed.

With an understanding of these 12 basic hues of the color wheel, you can begin to shift your thoughts toward dye mixing, as that is how to achieve custom colors. Remember, however, that using an artist's color wheel has its limitations, as the colors on the wheel are only approximate.

As a starting point, I have selected the Wash-Fast dyes Fuchsia (Red) 349, Blue 490, and Yellow 119 as the primary colors, but I would also suggest having black available to add for depth of shade. I find I can mix any color imaginable from the four colors I have suggested; it's possible to create any color by varying the hue, intensity, and value.

To get a more versatile range of colors, I often expand my color resources with several other dyes, such as Violet 817 and Turquoise 478. I use Red 351 to get a pure red, but haven't suggested using it as a primary color because it is difficult to mix with other dyes and because Fuchsia 349 makes it easier to obtain exciting colors.

As a dyer, you have to become familiar with how the WashFast acid dyes react when mixed together and to understand their specific characteristics and subtleties. For instance, each dye, whether straight from the dye jar or mixed with another dye, will adhere to the fiber at different rates. This makes it hard to determine your exact color early in the dyeing process; you have to wait for all the dye molecules to be fixed on the fiber to see the final color outcome.

Hues do not reach full saturation with equal amounts of dye; getting a true blue will take more dye than getting an intense yellow. Yellow is closer to white than the other two primaries and is therefore brighter; blue is closer to black and therefore darker. I have found that proportionally I use more yellow than any other dye when mixing colors. One of my favorites, chartreuse, takes 95 percent yellow and 5 percent blue. To make a nice coral, I use 90 percent yellow and 10 percent fuchsia.

The colors of a flower can suggest ways to mix vibrant tones for a special project.

Making Your Own Favorite Colors

Now comes the fun part. Once you have learned the basics, you can play. This is where your natural instincts come into view—yes, you do have them. As I stated in the chapter devoted to color, there are many ways to see it, feel it, design with it, and now, dye it. Curiosity and a sense of adventure are good things when you're learning something new. Invite a knitter or spinner friend over for a daylong adventure to learn to dye your own palettes. As I have stressed many times, color is about seeing and seeing is observing. Take the time to walk: find a meadow in springtime or an ice floe on a winter afternoon at sunset, and absorb the natural beauty that surrounds you. Maybe you might want to try to duplicate some of these colors in the dye pot. Subtle or bright, warm or cool, earth tones or jewels, colors make a statement in everything we do.

Over the years, I have found that I use some colors consistently in my palette, and I will share these personal favorites with you. Living in Maine, I am struck by natural beauty every time I step outside, and sometimes I don't even need to do that. I might look out my dye studio window and see the next color arrangement in front of me.

Here are some of my own dye formulas. These amounts of dye stock solution will dye 4 ounces (113g) of yarn in a dark shade or 8 ounces (227g) in a medium shade. (If the yarn you are using is in pull-skeins or on cones, make it into reeled skeins, as described on page 31.)

Dyeing the Yarn

Read the general instructions on how to dye yarn (pages 32–34). Follow the steps for wetting out the fiber, making dye solutions, and making the dye bath.

You have already begun the mixing and experimenting. If you haven't done so already, now is a good time to start keeping a notebook handy, so you can write down formulas and keep samples of your dyed yarns.

To Make	Use This Much Dye Stock Solution
Spring fern green	10 Tbsp (147.75ml) Yellow; 1 tsp (5ml) Blue
Mussel shell blue	6 Tbsp (89ml) Blue; 4 Tbsp (59ml) Black; 1 Tbsp (14.75ml) Red
Autumn leaf gold	12 Tbsp (180ml) Yellow; 2 Tbsp (29.5ml) Red; 1 tsp (5ml) Black
Lupine purple	4 Tbsp (59ml) Blue; 4 Tbsp (59ml) Violet; 2 Tbsp (29.5ml) Red
Evening sunset	8 Tbsp (118.25ml) Red; 3 Tbsp (44ml) Yellow; ¼ tsp (1.25ml) Black
Evergreen pine	6 Tbsp (88.75ml) Blue; 4 Tbsp (59ml) Yellow; 2 tsp (9.75ml) Black
Tbsp = tablespoon	**tsp = teaspoon**

■ HOW TO SPACE-DYE YARN

With space-dyed yarns, each skein is dyed with three colors. (Trying to use more than three colors can yield muddy-looking results.) Rather than being completely submerged in the dye bath, as for solid-color dyeing, the skeins are suspended so that only part of the yarn is in the bath as you dye each individual color. The colors are dyed in sequence, using the same water.

equipment

- 20-gallon (75-liter) stainless steel or enameled pot
- 3 plastic measuring cups
- Set of measuring spoons
- Plastic spoons
- Wooden stirring spoon
- Heavy plastic cups
- Wooden dowel 1'' in diameter and long enough to span the top of the pot
- Color wheel
- Dust mask
- Rubber gloves

materials

- Enough yarn for your project
- Sampler kit of WashFast acid dye, which includes Synthrapol SP and citric acid (available from www.pinetreeyarns.com)

Preparing the Yarn

If the yarn you are using is in pull-skeins or on cones, make it into reeled skeins, as described on page 31. If you are space dyeing more than one skein, and you want the knitting results to be consistent, all the skeins need to be of similar length so the color intervals will be consistent. You can dye up to four 4-ounce skeins (1 lb, or .45kg) at a time.

Wet out the fiber for at least an hour, or overnight for silk (see page 32).

Choosing your Colors and Preparing the Dye Solutions

Remember to put on your gloves and mask and review all the safety rules before you begin this process.

It is time to begin making the colors for your space-dyed skeins. Look at your color wheel and choose three compatible colors. You might also want to review my discussion of color harmonies before making your selection (pages 18–21).

Mix up your primary-color dye stock solutions and proceed to mix your chosen colors by following the directions on pages 32–38.

To test a color, use the plastic spoon to drop a small amount of mixed solution onto a white piece of paper. This will give you an approximate idea of what the color will look like when applied to the yarn.

∧ variety of space-dyed yarns make a great collage of color.

Planning the Dye Sequence

The sequence in which you use your three colors will affect how they evolve on the skeins. In general, it is a good idea to dye the lightest color first and the darkest color last.

Most of the time, one dye will be exhausted into the fiber and the dye bath will be clear before you move on to the next color, but this is not always the case. For instance, let's say you have chosen to space-dye chartreuse (yellow and a tad of blue), dark blue, and magenta. If you dye with magenta first, chartreuse second, and blue third, there might be a residue of magenta in the dye pot—some dye left unabsorbed by the fiber—that will affect the chartreuse color. (Actually, this can be part of the fun of dyeing your own yarn. It allows some mystery and fascination to enter the process.)

The second way colors will affect each other is when they merge together as you rotate the skeins on the dowel to dye the next color. Color A and color B will have a range of overlap as wide as you want it to be. In the area of overlap, you will get yet another color that is a combination of Color A and Color B. So the three colors you have selected will actually produce six colors on the skeins being dyed.

Dyeing the Yarn

The dyes have been mixed and you are ready to begin. For 1 or 2 skeins, fill the dye pot about one-third full with warm water. For 4 skeins (1 lb, or .45kg), fill the dye pot one-half full to be sure there is plenty of liquid so the skeins can move freely. Stir in the first dye solution. Insert the dowel into your wetted-out skeins. Place the dowel across the rim of the dye pot and lower the yarn into the dye pot so that only one-third of each skein is in the water. (If you have filled the dye pot to the halfway point, you may need to find a way to raise the dowel higher than the edge of the dye pot to ensure that only one-third of the yarn is submerged.)

Turn on the stove to medium heat, and bring the water to the desired temperature (212°F, or 100°C, for wool; 185°F, or 85°C, for silk, mohair, or cashmere). Turn down the heat and simmer for 15 minutes, or until the liquid in the pot looks clear and colorless. Lift the dowel once or twice to gently swish the yarn in the dye bath and ensure that the dye is being evenly distributed.

At the end of 15 minutes, lift the dowel with one hand and use the other hand to rotate the yarn one-third around to the next section to be dyed. Add the next color to the dye bath, stir it around, and lower the yarn back in the dye pot, making sure that there is some color overlap on the skein (no white is showing). Simmer for another 15 minutes.

Repeat these steps of rotating the yarn, adding dye, and simmering one more time.

Finally, after the last color has been used and the dye bath is clear and colorless, remove the

Once a color has been dyed, lift the dowel and rotate the skein so that the next third is in position to be dyed.

dowel and completely submerge the skeins in the water. Continue simmering for another 45 minutes to set the dye. Turn off the heat and allow the yarn to cool down while in the pot.

When the skeins are cool, rinse them in *lukewarm* water, squeezing them before hanging them on a dowel to dry. Your first space-dyed wool is now ready to be used.

Three colors have been dyed.

Add the next dye to the pot and lower the skein so that one-third of it is submerged in the dye bath.

■ HOW TO HAND-PAINT YARN

While trying to use more than 3 colors can lead to problems when you are space-dyeing, the hand-painting technique can yield beautiful results with as many as six colors applied to the same skein.

Hand-painting works well with many types of yarn. I often use a 2-ply gray ragg wool or Brown Sheep Company 1-ply sport or worsted weight wool. Some novelty yarns may not be suitable for hand painting, but mohair boucle, wool slub (Henry's Attic [HA] Periwinkle), textured wool (HA Mikado), and mohair/wool blend (HA Texas) are all fun to hand-paint. The results will be unpredictable yet beautiful. Silk is difficult to hand-paint because the fiber is dense and the dye has a hard time being absorbed into the fiber.

equipment

- 20-gallon (75-liter) stainless steel or enameled pot
- Measuring cups
- Stainless steel colander
- Enamel canning pot
- Measuring spoons
- 6 (2-cup; 500ml) plastic squeeze bottles
- Plastic spoons
- Wooden stirring spoon
- Color wheel
- Dust mask
- Rubber gloves
- Oven mitt

Hand-painted yarns look soft and sensual because of the way they are dyed.

materials

- Enough yarn for your project
- Sampler kit of WashFast acid dye, which includes Synthrapol SP and citric acid (available from www.pinetreeyarns.com)

Preparing the Yarn

If the yarn is in pull-skeins or on cones, rewind it into reeled skeins before dyeing (page 31).

Wet out the fiber according to the directions on page 32, stirring in 2 tablespoons of citric acid before immersing the skeins; this will help the dye affix to the fiber. **Hand-painting wool is like making a watercolor; the surface cannot be too wet or too dry.** This is critical, so feel the skeins to make certain that they are damp, not soaking wet or too dry. The yarn should feel like a damp washcloth. Put the wetted-out skeins into a plastic bag to keep them evenly dampened until you use them.

Preparing the Stock Solutions

Prepare the stock solutions as described on page s 32–33. (This can be done while you are waiting for the skeins to be wetted out.) Make several stock solutions with as many dyes as you wish.

Mixing the Colors

Now the creative fun begins. What do you want your hand-painted skein to look like? Are you thinking summer ocean blues or autumn reds and oranges? At this time I might take out my watercolors and pick out some colors to see how they blend together.

When hand-painting yarns I usually mix 6 colors to apply to the skein . I normally mix a yellow, several blues and greens, violet, magenta, and maybe orange. I do not use a dye solution right out of the jar but throw a bit of another color into the mix to make it unique.

To check the colors you have made and to see how they look together, put a small amount of each dye onto a white piece of paper. Do you have too many similar colors? One that doesn't work with the others? Too many dark shades? This process will give you a chance to see how the colors will look on the wool.

Put your new colors in separate plastic squeeze bottles (old ketchup bottles work fine), making sure to add enough warm water to make a 2-cup solution for each color. When mixing these colors, you may need to replenish the stock solutions to mix new colors.

Painting the Yarn

Prepare your working surface by putting down plastic sheets or newspaper. Arrange the selected dyes, in their plastic squeeze bottles, within easy reach. Lay your wetted-out skeins flat on the covered area, spreading out the yarn so you can work with the individual strands. Take the first bottle you want to use, hold it a foot above the skein, quickly tip it down, and pour a little dye on one part of the skein. Use a fast motion, because you do not want a lot of dye in one spot. Apply the color, using the same technique, in several places on the skein. **A light touch is good**—the color will spread as the dye migrates up the strands of yarn, so less is better than more.

Continue putting dye on the skein, using each of the colors, each color finding its own spot. When the first side of the skein has been painted, turn it over and use the same dyes in the same order to dye the other side. When you have finished, turn your skein, looking for spots you have missed, and paint these places.

Be careful not to saturate the skein in dye, or it will turn to mud colors as the areas of dye run together. It is better to allow white or gray fiber to show, as these spots may absorb dye from neighboring strands. (If undesired white spots remain, there are ways to correct this, as I discuss below.)

When you are happy with your skein, stop applying dye and let it be—leave it flat on the work surface. After one hour, check on it to see how it

When hand-painting yarns, mix several dye colors, pour a small amount of each dye solution on several places on the skein, and observe how the color moves along the strands.

Continue adding your varied colors to the skein, each color finding its own spot. They will magically blend together.

looks now that the dye has had time to flow and spread along the fibers. Are there spots that need a little more dye? At this stage there are two things you can do to correct colors. First, you can try adding a little more color randomly to the skein. If it looks flat, I often add yellow consistently throughout the skein so it will bounce the other colors. The second thing you can do is to gently squeeze the skein with your hands from end to end. This will make the colors bleed into one another, putting color through the entire skein and causing the white areas to disappear. Be careful when squeezing, because it will blend the colors so they may no longer be as individualized.

When you are happy with your yarn, cover it with plastic and let it sit for several hours or overnight.

Setting the Dye

Because WashFast acid dyes need heat to affix the dye to the fiber, you need to steam the yarn after it is hand painted.

To steam the wool, put water in the dyeing pot, or any size pot that a colander will fit on top of. Make sure the water level stays below the bottom of the colander. Bring the water to a boil, put 2 skeins in the colander, cover, and simmer the water. The heat from the steam will set the dye.

Set your timer for 15 minutes, and rotate skeins every 15 minutes until they have steamed for an hour altogether. The yarn will be very hot, so wear an oven mitt when rotating the yarn. After an hour, turn off the heat and allow the yarn to cool to room temperature.

Steaming the hand-painted skeins for an hour will set the dye into the fiber so it is washfast.

Rinse the skeins in lukewarm water and hang them to dry. Some excess dye might come out as the yarn is rinsed; if this happens, rinse it again until the water runs clear. I put the yarn on a dowel to dry, making sure to catch the dripping water in a bucket.

Many types of yarn fill the dye pot, and each fiber takes the dye differently.

■ DYEING DIFFERENT FIBERS TOGETHER (Textural Dyeing)

Working with several different types of fibers in the same dye pot can be fun and challenging. You can dye skeins of different fiber together or dye blended yarns. Each fiber in a blend—wool/angora, for example—will take the dye differently, so keep this in mind when selecting your fibers.

What if you have a yarn with both protein and cellulose fibers—or a mystery skein that is a blend of heaven knows what? Dye it! Since the WashFast acid dyes do not react with cellulose fibers, only the protein fiber in a blend will take up the dye, while the cellulose fibers remain unchanged. This can create very interesting and attractive results.

equipment

- 20-gallon (75-liter) stainless steel or enameled pot
- Measuring cups
- Set of measuring spoons
- Plastic spoons
- Wooden stirring spoon
- Color wheel
- Dust mask
- Rubber gloves

materials

- Enough yarn (of different types) for your project
- Sampler kit of WashFast acid dyes, which includes Synthrapol SP and citric acid (available from www.pinetreeyarns.com)

Preparing the Yarn

If the yarn is in pull-skeins or on cones, rewind it into reeled skeins before dyeing (page 31).

Wet out the fiber according to the directions on page 32, remembering that any yarn containing silk needs to be soaked overnight.

Preparing the Dye

Prepare stock solutions as described on pages 32–33. (This can be done while you are waiting for the skeins to be wetted out.) Mix the stock solutions to create your desired color, being sure to mix the dye thoroughly, otherwise the particles will randomly affix to the fibers at different times, causing different colors to be produced. (Unless this is the effect you want, then that's all right.)

Dyeing the Yarns

Fill the dye pot with water and add the dye mixture. Make sure you keep some of the mixture in reserve because you may need it later in the dyeing process. Follow the general directions for dyeing on page 34, remembering to not heat the dye bath above 185°F (85°C) when dyeing yarns containing silk or cashmere or mohair.

Put the wetted-out yarns into the pot one skein at a time, stirring the dye bath as you add them. Do this quickly because the dye will immediately begin to affix to the fiber, and you probably want a similar depth of shade on each skein.

You want all the dye to get on the yarns, which will happen at different times because each type of fiber has its own way of reacting to heat and dye. The variation among fibers is what makes textural dyeing so exciting.

Skeins of different fiber compositions in the dye bath, each absorbing the dye at its own rate and intensity.

The same skeins after completing the dye process. The cotton/rayon type (plant fibers) took very little dye while the protein fibers—mohair loop, silk, silk chenille, and wool boucle—took more color, each according to its nature.

As the dye bath heats up, you will see which skeins are dyed more intensely and which more unevenly. Some of the skeins, such as silk, might not take the dye evenly. Other skeins, such as angora or cashmere, will be lighter in color.

If an individual skein is unevenly dyed—most likely to happen when you're dyeing silk—you can add some of the reserved dye. Bring the problem skein to the top of the dye bath, pour some of the reserved dye solution into the dye bath, and stir gently. Allow an additional 15 minutes for the added dye to bond with the fiber.

Depending on how you want the fibers to work together in the finished product, you can even add a small amount of a different-color dye at the end to give the fiber some subtle color differentiations.

■ OVERDYEING YARN

Overdyeing is another way to play with color or use up yarn that needs a new life. You might have collected odds and ends of already dyed yarns that have been around for a long time; now they can be useful in a different project. With overdyeing, yarn will change color significantly.

Take several yarns of different colors and textures—light colored ones are best—and find a color that will work with them. If most of the yarns are neutral grays, you can overdye them using any color. If they are mostly blues or reds, you need to be careful to choose a color to enhance these primary colors. In any case, you will need to make a dye mixture that will yield a medium shade for the amount of fiber you are dyeing. (See pages 35–36 for information on dyeing different shades of color.)

When different types of yarn are overdyed together, each will have its own shade yet will blend in with the all the others in a unified and pleasing combination.

Preparing the Yarn

If the yarn is in pull-skeins or on cones, rewind it into reeled skeins before dyeing (page 31).

Wet out the fiber according to the directions on page 32, remembering that any yarn containing silk needs to be soaked overnight.

Preparing the Dye

Prepare stock solutions and mix your final desired dye color as described on pages 32–33. (This can be done while you are waiting for the skeins to be wetted out.)

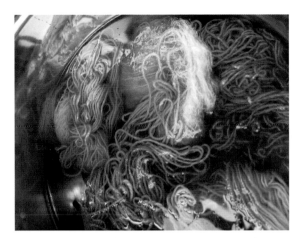

Overdyeing a mix of different yarns in the same dye bath can give unity to a multi-yarn project.

A beautiful family of yarns all overdyed with the same color.

Dyeing the Yarns

Follow the general directions for dyeing on page 34, remembering to not heat the dye bath above 185°F (85°C) when dyeing yarns containing silk or cashmere or mohair.

■ EXPERIMENTAL YARN DYEING

Being in the dye studio is always an adventure. At the moment, I share my studio with a fellow dyer, Lynne Wallace. Watching her transform white yarn into something interesting has opened my eyes to new possibilities. "Let's play," I suggest, as inventive dots of color become a polka-dot masterpiece. Lynne and I both relish the adventures of dyeing and finding our own ways of putting colors on fiber.

Learning to dye yarn is about you, the person who is standing in the studio, making colors happen on the skein. It can be fun, wild, sophisticated, or as tentative as you want the experience to be, depending on the day, the hour, and the mood you are in. Again, as I have stated many times, take the time to relax, to find a quiet moment, and think color. When I walk into my studio, I have found that I can never predict what is going to happen. I allow the experience to heighten my awareness of the kind of day it is outside, sunny or rainy, and how it can transform or exhilarate my mood, simply by mixing some colors together. The hustle-bustle of the outside world comes to a halt as I find new ways to interpret the color schemes around me.

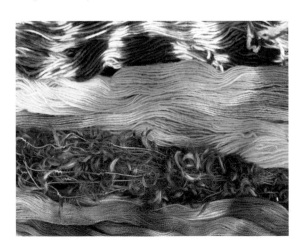

Experimental yarns . . . "Let's play!" Top to bottom: tie-dyed, rainbow-dyed, rainbow-dyed novelty yarn, squirt-dyed.

The next few pages contain some examples of new techniques invented on the spot as dye bottles and sprayers went to work on a white skein of yarn.

equipment

- 20-gallon (75-liter) stainless steel or enameled pot
- Measuring cups
- Stainless steel colander
- Measuring spoons
- 6 plastic squeeze bottles
- Spray bottles
- Plastic spoons
- Wooden stirring spoon
- Rubber bands or heavy string
- Color wheel
- Dust mask
- Rubber gloves
- Oven mitt

materials

- Enough yarn for your project
- Sampler kit of WashFast acid dyes, which includes Synthrapol SP and citric acid (available from www.pinetreeyarns.com)

Preparing Skeins and Dyes

For all of these experimental techniques, follow the basic directions for preparing dyes (pages 32–33) and wetting-out the fibers (page 32).

Polka dots appear as I squirt color on a skein of dyed wool.
(top right)

A randomly polka-dotted skein eagerly waiting to be knitted.
(lower right)

Polka Dots

I love my red polka-dot dress, and I love watching as polka dots just appear on a skein as I dye it. A polka-dot–dyed skein creates a knitted fabric with little one- or two-stitch flecks of color sprinkled here and there.

To achieve polka dots, first dye a skein a solid color, which should be light—such as pale yellow or pink—so the dots will show up. Follow the general dyeing directions on page 34.

When the cooled yarn comes out of the dye bath, spin it in the washing machine for a minute until most of the water is out of it. Lay the skein on a table covered with a plastic sheet or newspapers. The polka dots are squirted on with a spray bottle

Polka dot yarn

filled with some wild color (or several bottles with several colors). Let the yarn sit for an hour, and then steam it for 30 minutes to set the dye, as described on page 44.

Easy as pie.

Tie-Dye

The tie-dyed look of the 1960s comes back, with results that can look like snake or lizard skin, or an evening sky filled with fireflies, or Ikat gone crazy.

First, space-dye a skein of yarn using vibrant colors or earth tones, depending on the effect you want. You will be overdyeing some places, so don't make the space-dyed colors too dark. (See "How to Space-Dye Yarn," pages 39–41)

Spin the cooled yarn in the washing machine so it isn't too wet. Take rubber bands, plastic bobbins, or heavy string—whatever is handy that can resist the dye—and tie these things to the skein in as many places as you like. Alternatively, you can knot the skein in several places, as old-school tie-dyers

would do. Put the skein into a dye bath of a contrasting color or black and let it simmer for one hour.

Cool the skein and rinse it, then take off the rubber bands or untie the skein.

You can also do tie-dying in the reverse sequence by knotting the skein and dyeing it with one color, then untying it and space-dyeing over the first color.

Space-dyed yarn takes on a new dimension when it gets tied up with rubber bands and tie-dyed.

Elaine and Steve open the knotted areas of a tie-dyed skein and watch the colors unfold.

Tie-dyed yarn

Rainbow dyeing is a process of pouring pools of color onto the skein every few inches, producing a multicolored yarn.

Rainbow Dyeing

Rainbow dyeing is another form of magic, with colors flowing onto the fiber. Rainbow-dyed yarns are often called "hand-painted," but this technique really has more space-dyed qualities. It allows you to use more colors than space-dyeing alone, however—as many as seven or eight. (Remember, though, that using too many contrasting colors together in a skein can give your knitted fabric a muddy look.) In rainbow dyeing you also have a different kind of control over placement of colors.

Put a wetted-out skein (page 32) on a table and, using your squeeze bottles, put dye on in two- or three-inch sections along the skein. Some sections of color can be longer or shorter, giving a random effect. Be bold!

Let the dyed yarn sit for an hour, and then steam it for 20 minutes to set the dye, as described on page 44.

Jackson Pollock Effect

This technique was invented and designed for a friend of mine who wanted a certain look. It creates a lot of dye fumes, so be sure to follow safety precautions.

Mix dye solutions for four colors—for example, brown as the base, plus green, plum, and navy.

Take a wetted-out skein of bulky-type yarn and put it in the dye pot with very little water, just enough to cover the skein. Turn the heat on low. When the yarn is hot (212°F, or 100°C, for wool; 185°F, or 85°C, for silk or cashmere), pour each dye mixture onto the skein in sequence, using a lot of the main color first and then the others in different places to give it an overdyed look.

Do not stir. Let the dye pot simmer for 30 minutes. Turn the skein over to make sure both sides are exposed to the dye and simmer for 30 minutes more. Turn off the heat, let the skein cool, and rinse it in lukewarm water.

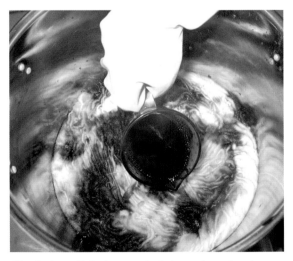

The Jackson Pollock-esque technique of pouring dye directly onto the skein.

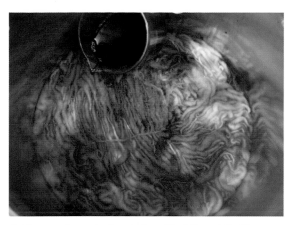

Add more dye onto the skein until all the white fiber disappears; watch the dye colors interact in an interesting way.

Squirt Method

Using squeeze bottles holding dye solutions in different colors, apply dye into the crevices and folds of a tightly wound skein of light-colored yarn that has been wetted out.

Steam the yarn, let it cool, and then open up the skein to see how the yarn has been transformed into a wild fiber.

Use the squirt method to apply the dye into crevices of a tightly wound skein that has been wetted out.

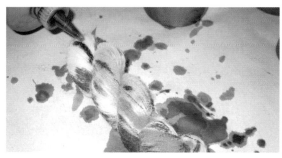

Watch how colors transform the skein as they spread.

Pollock yarn

Squirt yarn

For sprinkle dyeing, put tiny amounts of dry dye on a wet skein of yarn. Colors interact and learn to get along together throughout the dyeing process.

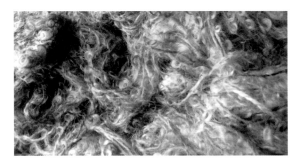

As the sprinkled yarn sits for an hour, the dry dye flows and is absorbed into the strands, producing an interesting array of subtle colors.

Sprinkle Dyeing

Be sure to wear your mask when handling the dye powders, and do not have a fan going or your windows open.

Wet out your skein using 1 tablespoon of citric acid and 1 teaspoon of Synthrapol in the water. (See "Wetting Out the Yarn," page 32.) Spread out the very wet skein in a large, shallow enameled or glass pan.

Randomly sprinkle dye powders in tiny amounts on the wet yarn, watching how they mingle. The colors will migrate along the strands, so be aware of overlaps.

Let the yarn sit for an hour, then steam it for 45 minutes to set the dye, as described on page 44.

Forget-the-Rules Method

Throw a skein of dry (not wetted-out) yarn into a dye bath and see how the dye goes onto the fiber unevenly, producing streaking—and striking—results. Do not stir the fibers until near the end of the dyeing process, and then throw more dye on the skein, maybe using another color.

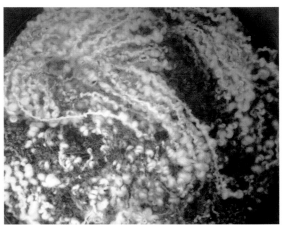

The "forget the rules" method gives you another chance to explore and experiment with dye by adding color to a dry skein of yarn. Fibers that have not been thoroughly wetted out accept dye in an interestingly irregular way.

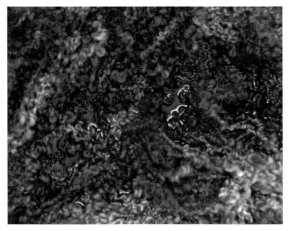

Layers of light and dark reds and purples flow together for a balance of color.

The many years I have been in the dye studio have shown me that happy mistakes do happen. Quite often I had no idea—in advance—of what I was doing, but knew that I wanted to try something different. Trying many different techniques over the years has become a way to focus on the creative process. It's fun to be inventive. Let your own sense of adventure blossom.

Skeins showing experimental dye techniques. Clockwise from upper left: rainbow dyed, forget the rules, squirt, sprinkle, Pollock, polka dot, and tie-dye.

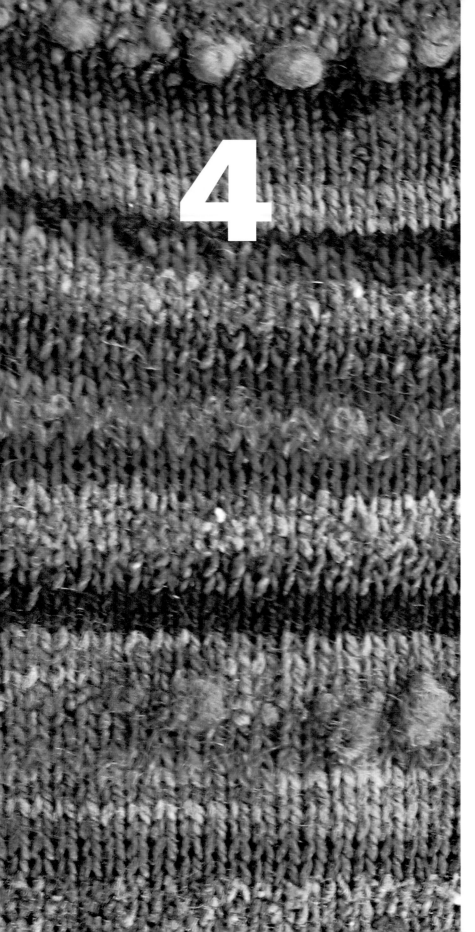

4

the Design phase

My knitting reflects who I am, how I view my world, and how I interact with the world around me. Every knitting project, no matter how small or large, is approached with the same passion. Knitting is my constant companion and allows me to freely express my mood, as it is part of a creative expression that lies within my soul. Beautiful fiber and familiar needles in my hands allow a sense of groundedness to run through me—I am home wherever I am. I write this while sitting on my garden terrace in Sicily, knowing that my stitches will help me focus on my thoughts and life here. It took me four weeks to pick out yarns to pack for this two-month sojourn—but just ten minutes to pack my clothes.

I do not do complicated knitting. I want to be able to pick up my project at any moment, settle down, and find a quiet place to reflect while those stitches are moving across the needles in their own rhythm. Life is busy enough with the everyday demands of family, work commitments, social interactions, and a busy store to run. We all have these

A charted stitch design worked in solid-dyed silk. Here, texture is used to bring out the pattern.

In this swatch, space-dyed yarn and solid wool were used to work the same charted design. This time, it's color rather than texture that makes the pattern.

This time, the design swatch was knit with hand-painted wool. Now color and texture combine for a third and completely different look, but note how the texture does not show up as clearly.

demands. I am going to ask you to set aside some time each day to find a quiet place to sit and knit and take a few moments to notice the textures and colors around you. It is here, when life around us slows down, that we can enable the creative process within us to find a happy way of being expressed. And then, finding our own ability to see and design our own patterns is not as terrifying as it might seem.

In this section of the book, I will focus on the three types of dyed yarn—solid-dyed, space-dyed, and hand-painted—and how to work with each of them in any project. But first, I need to talk about gauge (also sometimes called tension).

■ THE ALL-IMPORTANT GAUGE

Knitting is a process, and it starts with the almighty gauge. When a customer comes into my shop with a specific pattern for which he or she wants to find suitable yarn, the first words out of my mouth are, "What's the gauge and recommended needle size?" Every pattern will have this, and with this information in hand, we can begin to search for the right yarn suitable to the gauge. This begins the process of knitting a successful garment. I remind my customer that it is essential to actually do a test swatch and confirm that the gauge is accurate for the given project.

When someone first buys yarn from me for a pattern, I say, "As long as you have the yarn, I will help you with your project." I specifically have the gauge in mind as I make that offer, though often I end up helping with other aspects of the pattern as well. I get phone calls from all over the country, e-mails from around the world, and people coming into the shop daily to have me check out their progress. But that's what I want—communication.

And yet . . . most of my shop customers do not knit a gauge test swatch, even though I insist that it is important. Why? They tell me they usually knit to gauge, or they say they don't have time, and that they just want to get started on the project itself. This is fine until they come back to me days or weeks later with something that doesn't fit properly. I ask, "Did you do your gauge and measure it accurately?" But I already know the answer—they'll flinch and say no.

The gauge is the number of stitches and rows it takes to make a 4-inch (10cm) square of knitting. Every published pattern has this necessary information, and it is based on the gauge that was made by the designer. Everyone knits differently, so to suppose that you will knit *exactly* like the designer is to invite disastrous results. Every knitting pattern uses a different kind of yarn, stitch pattern, and needle size, and these also affect the gauge.

Your knitting may also vary depending on your mood, what time of day you are knitting, what is on your mind or on the TV, how many hours you have been knitting, or the kind of yarn you are using. If you think that your stitches might be unusually tight or loose on a particular test swatch, do another to make sure your gauge is accurate.

There are three reasons to do a gauge swatch, and in all cases a swatch is essential. **(1)** You need to be assured that the finished garment will fit. You won't accurately control the size of your finished garment unless you know the gauge and therefore the number of stitches you will need to cast on. **(2)** You may want to alter the pattern, or perhaps you chose a weight of yarn that does not fit the original gauge. **(3)** If you start with your own original design, you need to determine the gauge so you can accurately create your envisioned project.

In all of these cases, we are talking about numbers. I, for one, am no mathematician, and was astonished when I learned, out of necessity, to do math at this late stage of my life! But the math is simple: the number of stitches per inch times the width of your project will give you the number of stitches to cast on.

If you are following a pattern, do the gauge swatch as suggested, using the recommended needles. If the gauge is 20 stitches to make a 4-inch (10cm) square, cast on 24 stitches so you have 2 extra stitches at each edge for easier measuring. Work the specified pattern stitch for 5 inches (12.5cm) and loosely bind off. (Remember to use the same type of needles for the gauge test that you will be using for the finished product; metal needles slide the yarn differently than wood needles, and that will affect the gauge.)

Lay your knitted gauge swatch flat on a table (not on your knee), use your tape measure or gauge tool to measure 4 inches or 10cm, and mark with pins. Count the number of stitches between the pins and compare that to the stated gauge for the pattern. Hopefully, the numbers will match, and you can begin your new project.

If your gauge doesn't match the one in the printed pattern, you have two options. The first is to

Counting stitches per inch to check your gauge can be a challenge when your swatch was knit with boucle or other highly textured yarn. Instead, you need to start with a known number of stitches and measure the width of the entire swatch.

change the needle size: if your swatch was smaller and used more stitches per inch, go up a needle size and try again. If the gauge was larger than specified, go down a needle size. Keep adjusting the needle size until you get the right number of stitches. Even half a stitch per inch, if multiplied by 20 inches (50cm), will make the finished garment too big or too small.

If you are not satisfied with the look of your gauge swatch—if the knitted fabric ends up being too open or too dense once you match the original gauge, it's probably because you are using a yarn that is heavier or lighter than the one used by the original designer. Your second option, then, is to find the gauge that suits *your* yarn and work the math to find out how many stitches to cast on for your desired garment size. To do this, multiply the number of stitches per inch (in the optimum gauge) by the width of your project, which will give you the number of stitches to cast on. You probably will also have to adjust the number of rows as well, so

be sure to check both your stitch gauge and your row gauge.

If you have some wonderful fuzzy yarn, such as mohair, that makes it difficult to count the stitches, make your sample swatch bigger than 4 inches or 10cm square. Measure the swatch and divide the number of stitches in the swatch by the width in inches, and this gives you the number of stitches per inch. You can use this method for any kind of novelty yarn or to determine any gauge that you will use in a project.

One word of caution here: as important as the test gauge is, it is not foolproof. I recommend to all my knitters, especially when they are attempting a challenging pattern stitch, that they measure the garment several times as the knitting progresses. As I said earlier, the gauge can vary with your own circumstances, so an accurate gauge needs confirmation, and the way to do this is to keep measuring! Hold the garment up to the wearer's body to see if it fits, or borrow a favorite sweater of theirs to compare the size.

A hand-dyed rainbow of colors create a sweater for a young child.

■ DESIGNING WITH HAND-DYED YARNS

Knitting with color has to do with your own eye and the confidence you have—or don't have—when putting colors together. It can be an exhilarating experience or one that exasperates you and puts you in a tizzy. There are many ways to build confidence and understanding when putting colors together. Mostly it is a matter of practice—putting together colors that you have in your stash of leftovers, watching for new yarns that excite you, rearranging the colors, or substituting a bright hue for a lighter shade. It is a very subjective process; there is no right or wrong way to do it. Play with the colors, make lots of swatches, and get a feel for how they settle with one another.

Picking out colors for any project, small or large, is the most confusing part of the design work. How you see color is an important aspect in this process. We are all programmed to think that some colors look good on us, or that a certain color, such as red, might evoke a reaction or mood change. We might associate a color with some memory: a school color or the smell of a flower. These things all come into play when we reach for a color and decide to work with it—or see it and reject it. Fortunately, there are no rights or wrongs when choosing colors, but it is a process that takes some getting used to. It takes time to figure out how color works. Working with many different colors in a project means making choices about which colors enhance or detract from one another. Sometimes it's simply rearranging the selected colors into a new colorful sequence. Sometimes substituting one color for another will make all the difference.

In the previous chapter, I discussed how to dye colors; now is the time to discover how to design with these colors. I will take you on a short journey to stimulate you and help you venture into the beautiful realm of color. I will also discuss the sources of color exploration that are so real and so important to my own sense of color.

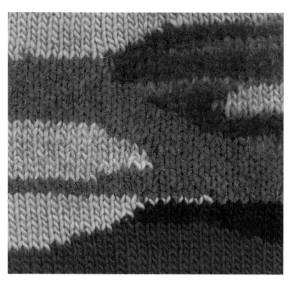

Using mostly solid dyed wool, I knit a swatch inspired by the colors in a Sicilian tile on my terrace.

Solid-Dyed Yarns

Let's start with where you are.

This is where I am. . . . I am looking at the Sicilian tiles on my terrace. I have twelve balls of yarn picked out to knit the colors of the tiles. This is my third try and still no luck. What am I doing here, and why is it not working? I am making it too complicated. I have beautiful colors arranged in a basket in front of me. I look at the subtle—and not so subtle—color changes in one tile and concentrate on just that tile. I am using solid-dyed wool this time. I will just enjoy putting the colors together as I normally do; that's when the magic happens. Cast on 25 stitches and knit. It's easy.

If you have shied away from colorful knitting that you invent as you go along, you can attempt it now. Solid-color hand-dyed wool, silk, mohair, or any other fiber can be visualized in a project because what you see is what you get. It's simply a matter of experimenting with the different attitudes of the yarns to achieve satisfying combinations. Begin by looking at the color wheel and select opposites, such as orange and blue, to produce a color combination in a pattern that pleases you. Starting with complementary colors will give you a sense of how two or more colors enhance and interact with one another. You can then expand your palette by adding more colors that will balance the warm-cool complementary-color combination. As a subjective starting point, remember color harmony—the theory of how colors work together.

My reaction to a color sequence might be totally different from yours. Practice is the best teacher here. Begin with colors that please you, either complementary or analogous; pick out five or more colors and line them up in front of you—or use a basket, as I do.

This is where the fun begins. You can move the balls in all directions until you get a sequence that pleases you. Then it's time to pick up your knitting needles and make a swatch. (A design swatch is a piece of knitting approximately 4 inches by 4 inches or 10 centimeters square.) Cast on 25 stitches with one color and knit several rows of garter stitch so the piece will lie flat. Then knit several rows of stockinette stitch with the same color, cut the yarn, and start with the next color. Do some seed stitches for texture. Keep adding new colors every few rows, changing the sequence as necessary. Abandon the judgmental side of yourself and let the process open up new possibilities. Keep knitting even if you are

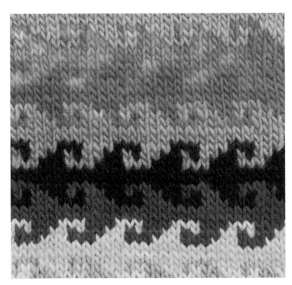

Complementary colors bring together coolness and warmth and enhance one another. Add as many colors as you like and experiment.

Adding a new yarn every few rows when experimenting with color will ensure that you never get bored with a project again.

not sure that you like the first few rows; sometimes you need to wait and see what the colors will do.

Unfortunately, we don't always like the results of our first attempts at selecting color. Some color combinations that look great in the basket just don't look right when knitted together. How you see the color may be totally different once the design or color combination is actually knitted. We can only continue to knit additional colors and experiment.

Working with colors is just a matter of choice. My own philosophy is, when in doubt, add 20 more colors. The colorist Kaffe Fasset, who revolutionized color knitting in the 1980s with his book *Glorious Knits*, initiated this concept. As I keep saying, there are no "right" answers here. Look on your design swatches as an introduction to color exploration. Every swatch does not need to be turned into a finished design. Once you have created several swatches that are pleasing to your eye, you will have a better sense of how *you* view colors together.

What's next?

There are many ways to put your dyed yarns together. First of all, I am not a stickler for using only similar weights and textures together in the same project. My sense of color and design comes from experience, luck, occasional fudging, and the belief that everything will turn out fine. I didn't always feel that way. When I started knitting, 50 years ago, I started with one color and one weight of yarn for each project. Many of us at that time viewed knitting as a final project made from a pattern and yarn, not as a process of changing colors many times during the actual knitting. While in college, I spent countless hours knitting a heathered blue Shetland sweater for a boyfriend, finishing the sleeves at midnight on Christmas Eve. Learning something new takes time. Time is a luxury—we don't always have enough or give enough time to ourselves.

So, although the hand-dyed skeins you make or buy are certainly going to be beautiful and interesting enough to be used alone in a project, you should also feel free to combine yarns of many textures, colors, and weights, if that's where your fancy leads you. Select silk, mohair, cotton, or anything that is

Try different textures. What does a silk yarn look like next to a mohair yarn?

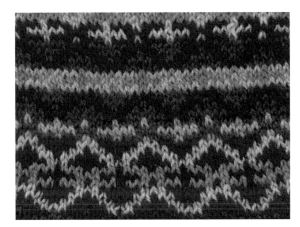

Patterns bounce as the you use colors from different areas of the color wheel, creating freshness in the design.

in your stash. What will you do with all this yarn?

Pick out six balls that you like and think might work together. Make a swatch trying different textures, using a needle size that is compatible with most of the yarns. Try making uneven stripes, using four rows of one color, three of another—I don't usually knit just one row or the color may get lost (unless it's from the yellow family). How does one texture fit in with the next one? How does a mohair look near a silk? I can tell you that mohair is usually finer and fluffier while silk is heavier and denser, but why not see for yourself what these fibers will do when knitted.

If you have the time, make five different striped swatches, just for the fun of it. At this point, if you are tired of doing swatches and want to make a project, pick out a simple pattern and put into practice some of the things you have already learned about color and texture. Try Emily's Baby Sweater (page 80) using lots of colors, or try knitting a scarf where the rows of knitting run lengthwise rather than crosswise.

Once you have played with simple stripes of solid color, it is time for a new challenge: patterns with color. Find or make up a simple chart that uses two or more colors. I usually only allow two colors at a time in each row, but I will change colors whenever and wherever I like. There are some simple guidelines to follow, but I want to emphasize that this book is not about rules. I want you to put colors together in your own way and, most important, enjoy the process.

You might want to knit a swatch with a two-color pattern using a hue's tone, tint, or shade. A sequence of values can be made using three or more colors going from light to dark. In most charted patterns there is a background color and a pattern color—use these to try different color combinations, such as bold and striking opposites or muted pastels and neutrals.

After trying out some simple color patterns, you may be inspired to look at Fair Isle designs and try some of those colorful arrangements. Although the charts look intricate, they call for working with only two colors on any given round or row.

When working with two-color knitting, you'll find that colors look different knitted together than they did when you held the individual balls of yarn side-by-side. One color might dominate while the other recedes, providing an unbalanced color arrangement. When you are working with contrasting values, remember that a color will look lighter against a darker background and darker against a lighter background. Also, if a warm color, such as pink, is juxtaposed with a cool color, such as blue,

These textures were created by combining knit and purl stitches worked in several solid-color dyed yarns.

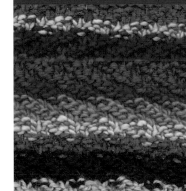

TEXTURE TOO!

Textured knitting is another way to expand your horizons, and the rhythm of the stitches can be satisfying as you knit. Solid-color yarns with a smooth finish are particularly well suited for working patterns with an interesting stitch texture. Some, such as lacework or cables, are traditionally done in one color, while others, such as the garter stitch chevron, require two or more colors.

You can also add a few "colorful" textures to your color experimentation, of course; it can be as easy as a two-color K2P2 ribbing. However, when you are combining a lot of different yarns in one project, it's usually not worth the effort to also toss in fancy cables and stitch patterns too, because they'll be camouflaged by all the other exciting visual things going on.

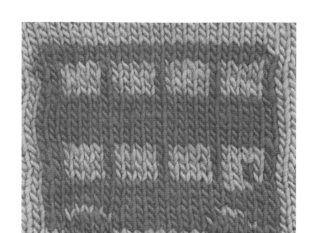

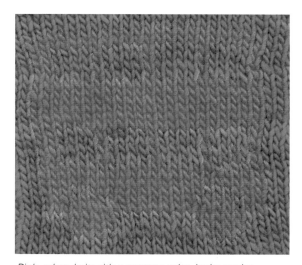

Pink, when knit with a warmer color, looks cooler. Knit against the backdrop of a cool color, pink will appear warmer.

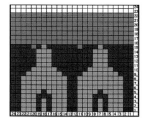 

A printed chart is two-dimensional and flat, while its knitted counterpart shows depth. Note the skyward-pointing "roof tiles" on the church and steeples.

the original pink will look even warmer. The same pink worked together with a warmer color, such as orange, will look cooler.

The size of the pattern components can also influence how the colors relate to one another. In a large pattern, the colors will retain their original characteristics; in a small pattern, the same colors are likely to melt into a muted effect and look like one blended color.

On a two-dimensional, flat pattern chart, the colors are individual colored squares; knitting adds a new dimension because yarn has depth. Stitches are not flat but lofty. The v-shaped stitches take on a life of their own and cast shadows where one color meets another. The knitted fabric will show the imperfections of how each stitch appears next to the other—especially when carrying several colors across a row.

Knitting books and magazines offer us specific instructions for patterns to use in our knitting projects. I want to help you find the confidence to try this on your own. I am not a knitwear designer, and I respect those individuals who come up with beautiful new patterns. Opening any guide to knitted stitches gives me hours of entertainment; there are so many ways that knit and purl stitches and combinations of colors can be arranged to make unique patterns. Many inspiring examples can be found in places such as *The Harmony Guide of Knitting* or Alice Starmore's wonderful *Charts for Colour Knitting*. Even at our most creative, we build upon stitch patterns that have been handed down through the ages. By bringing in our own original touches we individualize our finished pieces.

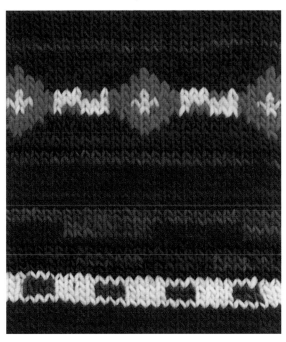

A Sicilian rug invited me to put these colors together.

As you continue to experiment, remember to seek out new, intriguing color combinations by looking around your natural world. I also love the colors in kids' artwork, Impressionist art, stone walls, and handcrafted materials such as tiles and textiles. I'll say more about sources of inspiration later in this section, but now that we've looked into doing creative things with solid-color yarns, let's move on to space-dyed and hand-painted yarns.

Space-Dyed Yarns

The availability of so many new multicolored yarns has made knitting popular again. New knitters gravitate to the exciting colors, wanting them all, while some seasoned knitters like what they see but don't know what to do with these new yarns. Eager as you might be to start working with a skein of yarn you just bought, you first need to know what

it is. Many techniques can produce a skein of multicolored wool, and the shopkeeper might not always know how it was dyed. It may be up to you to figure that out so that you can make something with it. Dip-dyed, rainbow-dyed, space-dyed, variegated, hand-painted, dyed in the roving and then spun, multistranded—these are all ways to make a multicolored yarn. All of these yarns can look yummy in the skein, as the beautiful colors jump out at you, but if you aren't careful, the unusual color scheme in the skein becomes a muddled mess when knitted. Who wants unsightly blotches of colors that randomly change or stripes that are not appealing to the eye?

That's why it is so important to take your beautiful multicolored yarn and figure out how the colors repeat. Some space-dyed skeins show the colors plainly, while some are not so obvious. If you have space-dyed the wool yourself, you will see the repeats clearly. When you cannot immediately discern the repeats in a skein that may have gotten jumbled or rewound, try taking several yards of the yarn, beginning with the end, and loop it around in

The colors look fantastic in the skeins, but how will this sampling of space-dyed yarns knit up? That's the mystery.

a big circle until the colors are lined up. Keep circling the yarn in this manner, trying to locate repeats, continuing to align the color sequence. How many colors are there? How are they repeated? If the colors change every few inches, you will work with the yarn differently than if the color intervals extend for 10 inches or more.

Now what do you do with it?

So many types yarn are available these days, and it isn't always easy to visualize what a given yarn will do, even after you have figured out the color repeats. Some of the new products on the market, like the Regia sock yarn, clearly state on the label how the yarn will work up. If you follow these instructions and get the correct gauge, you should be able to duplicate the pattern. If you are lucky enough to have a yarn shop nearby, there might be knitted samples on display. Then, based on how the colors look in the samples, you can decide what you like.

Space-dyed yarn works well when there are longer repeats, which you can ensure when you dye your own. Always bear in mind, though, that space-dyed yarn has a mind of its own—you can let it do what it wants to do naturally, or you can plan for it to do something specific in a pattern. You have several choices.

First of all, I rarely knit a project with only a space-dyed yarn. It is fine to work with it alone for small things, such as hats or mittens, or for something that is a simple, consistent shape—a scarf or shawl. But it gets complicated to work with it in a sweater. Once you decrease for the armholes, the color pattern will change, because from then on

you'll be working across a smaller number of stitches. The upper portion of the body will look different from the wider lower portion, and the sleeves will look different from the body. It becomes messy.

The color sequence of space-dyed yarn creates a spiral as the width of the knitted piece increases, altering the way the color intervals line up.

Space-dyed yarns create attractive spiral patterns in circular knitting, as in the Beret on pages 98–99. You can plan on a spiral pattern by knitting a certain number of stitches that add up to the repeat of the yarn's color sequence. Then you can add or subtract a few stitches to make the spiral or zigzag go to the right or the left.

Note that knitting a flat test swatch will *not*

show you how color placement will look in a hat or baby sweater knit in the round. In flat knitting, the color sequence will reverse as you work back and forth, and every other row will repeat itself in some kind of stripe effect. Therefore, it is important to recognize that the same space-dyed yarn will yield a totally different look when knitted flat than when knitted circularly.

Again, learning to see what the multicolored yarn will do takes time, lots of test swatches, and plenty of experimentation. Try making a swatch using a solid background color and space-dyed yarn for the pattern stitches. (Use a chart pattern in which the space-dyed yarn comes up several stitches at a time, so the color has an impact.) This technique works well because the space-dyed yarn gives the appearance that you have carried lots of colors, when in fact it's just the yarn changing colors as it is knit. Try reversing the technique: use the space-dyed yarn as the background and the solid color yarn for the pattern stitches. You will see dramatically different effects in how the colors look. You can knit a pattern as an accent to a project, to give it some nice color detail work.

Remember that although test swatches are always a good idea, their usefulness is limited when it comes to space-dyed yarns. For one thing, the color juxtapositions in a flat-knitted swatch will be different from those in an item knitted in the round. Also, exactly how the bands of color will interact depends on the total width of your piece of knitting; the color interactions in a 6-inch-wide swatch will not be the same as in an 18-inch-wide sweater back, even when both are made from the same skein.

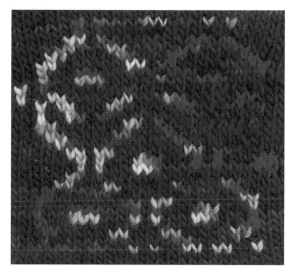

Used as the contrast color, the space-dyed wool creates a multi-colored effect, making it appear that you've used many different yarns instead of just two. Another little bit of magic.

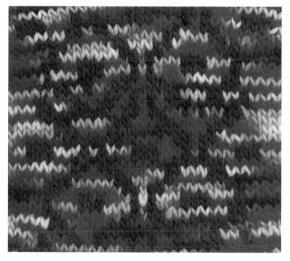

Space-dyed wool is used in the background in this two-color design, letting the blue wool pattern jump out.

Textured knitting is another way to use multicolored yarns, and working in something other than plain stockinette can help break up or disguise undesired stripey or blobby effects when you are using space-dyed yarns. For example, lace knitting can bring a new flow to how the colors run into

Space-dyed wool and an interesting stitch pattern combine to create a colorful rhythm.

Space-dyed wool happily changes colors every few stitches in this Nordic stitch pattern.

Subtle color changes can be achieved when knitting an intricate pattern with space-dyed yarns.

each other, especially if you use big needles. Certain stitch patterns, such as the double woven stitch or the oblique-knit rib, will give your eye the chance to blend the rhythm of the colors alongside the rhythm of the stitch pattern. Many of these techniques allow a random effect, so the space-dyed color repeats are not noticeable yet the colors continue to sing when knitted. Finding ways to emphasize the color changes without producing unsightly stripes is a challenge, but I have found that texture adds a lot to the form and bounciness of color repeats. Try two-color knitting, with a texture that uses a slip stitch to move the colors along in a dramatic way.

It's also an eye-opener to make swatches using different needle sizes—trying much larger or much smaller needles than you ordinarily would. This changes the denseness of the fabric, giving you more options for what you can make with your yarn.

Always make sure you have enough yarn to complete your project. Trying to dye more yarn or work out a solution when you don't have enough yarn will give you a reason to be either inventive or desperate. Most of the time, I use space-dyed yarn in projects that call for ten or more kinds of yarn; therefore, the amount I need is not so critical.

If you plan your project carefully when designing with space-dyed yarn, you can achieve wonderful results—just be patient in figuring out how to work with it and allow yourself plenty of time to experiment. Later in the book, I give some successful patterns using space-dyed yarn, and you can build upon them as you experiment further with colors and textures.

Hand-Painted Yarns

Hand-painted yarn has a casualness to it. There are no abrupt color changes, nor will there be a repeating color sequence. Because of the random, subtle color changes, this yarn can turn into anything without much effort. The flowing of colors into one another has to do with how the skein was dyed, like a watercolor full of rich hues. The colors can just be there for you. You don't have to do anything but notice—putting hand-painted yarn into a design is easy. Watch all those colors move through your fingers as you wind the skein into a ball, then pick up your needles and start knitting.

Looking at the skein will give you an idea of what is in store for this yarn. Does it have many, many hues, creating a richness from the colors working together? Or does it remind you of something specific: a field of lupines or the wings of a butterfly? I use hand-painted yarn when I am trying to create a mood or when I want its earthy qualities for a particular knitting project.

Like an accent in an evening sunset, hand-painted yarn can be part of a larger ensemble, used

Subtle colors in the hand-painted wool are brought to life by a black background in this houndstooth pattern.

A field of lupines shines after a spring rain.
Nature's gifts amaze me.

Lupines inspired the colorway of this hand-painted wool,
now knitted into cables in a hat.

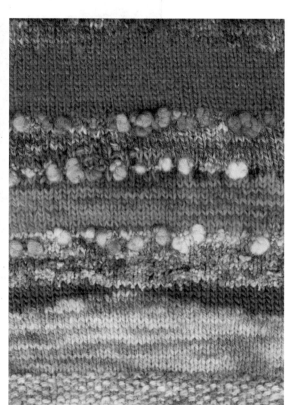

Hand-painted wool put to use in a vest that was
inspired by a tide pool at sunset.

in combination with various other muted and bright colors. Hand-painted yarn enjoys being used with other colors that make it stand out and be noticed. For instance, it is the focal point of the Maine Bounty sweater (page 110): one skein of hand-painted wool ties together all the other colors and textures and adds consistency and depth to the knitted fabric. The sweater would not work without this yarn; it becomes the part of Maine's bounty you notice while taking a walk or viewing a mossy forest floor. It gives the project definition because it has the allure of our natural surroundings.

Hand-painted yarn also works well all on its own because the colors stay soft and muted when knitted up. The gentle color transitions make every stitch a pleasure to knit. Try making up a skein into a pair of mittens or a warm scarf. The knitted mittens on page 107 show the softness, yet vitality, of the hand-painted colors working together.

So put a skein of hand-painted yarn in your hands and sit with it for a few moments. How would you like to use it?

The feel of hand-painted mohair in my hands . . . I look at the colors, subtle. They go from salmon-orange to rose to ochre to light lavender. The skein talks to me and says, "I want to be the texture of a Sicilian terrace tile."

YARN IN HAND
Six Knitting Designers Share Their Inspirations

 **Bill Huntington**

Owner of Hope Spinnery
Hope, Maine

I gave Bill a selection of beautiful earthy neutrals and shades that are seen in the natural world.

I use color in ways that seem natural to me. That may mean some abrupt changes of hue but mostly subtle shifts from shade to shade. In this piece, the foreground and the background each evolve and have a story to tell of a place, a thought, a motion. Sometimes they come close together and almost get lost in each other; at other times they stand out as bold individuals. Though the dark and light colors change every two rows, there is hardly any feeling of striation.

The wave seems to express a wonderful feeling of motion and stability at the same time. The image was plucked out of a larger scene and repeated to make a pattern reminiscent of a Japanese print. When drawn out, the pattern is bold and forceful. When knit in vibrant flowing colors, the pattern becomes less powerful but holds together the movement in a rhythmic play. If the piece were larger, the pattern may have been more eye-catching but here it is a subtext for the natural colors.

Jean Guirguis

Senior Editor of *Vogue Knitting*

I gave Jean four different textures—silk, mohair boucle, alpaca, and merino wool— that were all dyed at the same time.

Hand-dyes are my all-time favorite. The yarn does all the talking, transforming simple pullovers and cardigans into sophisticated yet very wearable works of art. The beauty of this hand-dyed yarn lies in the subtle tones and textures it produces as you knit. From frothy mohairs to crimped merinos and satiny silks, each fiber takes to dyes a little differently, producing one-of-a-kind results.

▪ Libby Mills
Green Mountain Spinnery
Putney, Vermont

I gave Libby two skeins, a hand-painted wool and a solid color dyed wool, that would provide some interaction when knitted.

What did I think about and feel as I worked this swatch?

First, of course, is the sense of wool on the fingers—good solid stuff, "real yarn," which I'd known as fleece before it was spun at the Green Mountain Spinnery.

And then there was the fun of watching the colors change in the hand-painted skein—"What's next?"

was the question hovering in my mind.

As for the swatch: working a Fair Isle pattern, I imagined first that the swatch would replicate a formal garden with a geometric design of many col-

ors. As I knitted on, my mind somehow turned to the memory of Fourth of July fireworks—bombs bursting in the sky, scattering rosettes of color.

▪ Prudence Mapstone
Author of *Freeform: Serendipitous Design Techniques for Knitting and Crochet*

I gave Prudence twelve skeins of interesting textures and vibrant colors in many different weights, some space-dyed, to allow lots of color to move around.

I believe that nobody should be afraid of color, and that we all have an innate color sense if we just allow ourselves to look closely enough at our work.

In selecting the yarns for each of the swatches that I worked, I moved the sample yarns around, adding to or taking away from the separate piles until I was happy with the various color combinations. I find that with my style of freeform knitting and crocheting, it is often possible to get even quite diverse colors to blend together well. This is probably partly because I

prefer to use each yarn for just a very small area of work each time, and partly because I like to alternate the smooth and the textured yarns, which definitely helps to soften the divisions between the color changes.

Once I am happy with my color selection, I then allow the composition of each yarn to dictate which stitches would be the best to showcase it. Therefore, I will generally use

just the plainest of stitches with textured or novelty yarns or with more involved color combinations, and opt for fancy stitches with the smooth yarns or more solid colors. Because my samples included some pure wool single-ply yarns, I worked these into crochet bullion stitches—this type of yarn really shows up that particular stitch to its best advantage.

Rick Mondragon

Editor of *Knitter's Magazine*

I gave Rick a selection of experimentally dyed wools, space-dyed, and solids with lots of textures and color to work with.

The yarns I was presented with were interesting because the textures and content were different in each. I like that. The challenge was the colors. I loved the lime and the teal; the variegated two were a bit too candylike for me. Although they worked well with the lime, I worried about using the teal, but it needed a contrast.

I strove to balance the teal and the lime as backgrounds in a 4/2/6 stripe repeat. I then knit the pattern with dashes of variegated, placed between each pair of rows. I worked a K3, slip 3 repeat across and a P3, slip 3 back, and in the following variegated rows the dashes shifted. I also changed from the variegated ribbon to the mohair after each staggered pair of dashes.

The body fabric has a lot going on: stripes in an undulating stripe sequence, slip stitch accents that change from fuzz.

I decided that the rib/trim should be a bit more angular/geometric and worked blocks. You can see that the teal is used in smaller blocks, as it is pretty powerful among the other colors.

I see a garment with a ribbed lower torso and a bodice of the dashed and striped fabric. I always sample the body fabric of a sweater first and add the trims later, as I did in this swatch. I find it an exciting way to create something unexpected.

Pam Allen

Editor of *Knits Magazine*

I gave Pam a dyed silk that was a soft grey-green overdyed with a hint of lavender, showing subtle color differences on the skein.

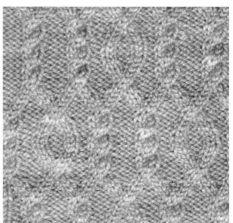

The subtle tonal colors of this silk yarn lend themselves well to textural patterns. I chose to experiment with cables whose twists are readily visible—the pattern doesn't get lost in the varying shades of color within the yarn. Equally important, these small twisting cables don't compete with the color pattern of the yarn.

The movement of the cable "ropes" also accentuates the slight sheen of this yarn.

Looking at a beautiful painting provides ideas on how colors can go together. (The Red Wagon, by Edith Haworth, author's collection)

■ SOURCES OF INSPIRATION

Artists

My Uncle George lives around the corner from New York's Metropolitan Museum of Art, so I was exposed to the art world at an early age. Without thinking much about it, I brought my own children to many museums around the world and around the corner, from the Topkapi in Istanbul to the Portland Museum of Art in Maine. Creating your own artwork and seeing the great artists' palettes and brushstrokes go hand in hand. Again, the operative word here is *seeing*. Find a painting or several paintings to provide a mood and a statement on how colors go together. The palette of Rembrandt is very different from that of an Impressionist. (My daughter Robin teaches art history, so I'd better be careful here.) Swirls of color on a canvas or thousands of tiny colored dots make a statement and give you information about how colors move in a

bold or diffused way. There might be only four apparent colors on a canvas, but take a look at the depth and layers of those colors. How do the colors and shapes work together?

Again, I stress time and awareness. Take some time to travel to your local art center, gallery, art museum, bookstore, or library, and see for yourself how an artist puts colors together. You don't have to be an art critic or scholar, but you do need to be exposed to the world of art. This is one route to seeing colors in a fresh way, and there is no training necessary. If you want to dye your own yarn or design a garment of many colors, the masters can be influential and inspirational. I spend hours looking at a painting, and every time I see it, it gives me something new to see—and it might also give me an idea for a color sequence or design.

If you don't have art books at home, go to the library and check out a book on the Impressionists or on one specific artist. Don't look at textbooks of art history; look for volumes that concentrate on quality reproduction paintings, books that present the artwork and the world of color, the artist's palette. You will have your own favorite artists, and I will share with you some of mine. They have all helped shape my color sense, my mood on a given day, and my confidence to visualize and obtain a creative outlet in knitting.

Artists have the awareness of color theory at their fingertips and understand the fundamentals of color mixing. They use this skill to expand their palette. Viewing a painting, one can focus on a variety of things: mood, light, texture, composition, brushstrokes, subject matter, color, and shape. How does the artist express these things? There is an emotional depth to each painter that goes beneath the brushstrokes of the work and discloses a sliver of his or her life view.

Here are some of my thoughts about favorite artists.

Mark Rothko

What draws me to Rothko? His study of color. The illusion of something that looks simple yet is so complex—but isn't hard to translate into a knitting pattern. Work his lines into a graph and knit inch by inch. It's the proportion that counts—the sense of the whole piece and how it is with the individual parts.

I love to study his color combinations, the layer upon layer of paint, how he uses primary colors in a subtle, sophisticated way. I also like his compositions of red and blue in different values. He has many dark canvases, but I also see the pure joy of

A Rothko painting inspired this simple design for a pillow.

his pink, orange, lime green, and yellow canvases, which bring in so much light. Layers and balance, lots of horizontal lines—what can I do with them to make a knitting design? I love working within his layers of colors because I can achieve as much depth or simplicity in the piece as there is time available for the project.

Finding the right yarn is the key, as the translucency that is so apparent in Rothko's work needs to be expressed in the knitted piece as well. Some silk, some blended textiles, some way, maybe through the stitches, to obtain that depth of color—that's the challenge.

I have made six or more designs based on Rothko's work; one, the Rothko Pullover, is included in this book (page 84). I relate to his color fields, the autonomy of his close color harmonies, the unity and strength of each large canvas. Looking at his creations, I am engulfed in an aura of color that surrounds my soul and grounds me.

Pierre Bonnard

The playful brushstrokes of color in Bonnard's work reveal a lot of texture and remind me of my knitting. They form color blocks that can easily be translated into a knitted fabric. Bonnard's colors are warm and sensual—lots of oranges, yellows, and violets. I study the fluidity of how one area of color moves into another within a context of different brushstrokes. Bonnard is a master at magnificently balancing the warm and cool colors. He brings your eye into inviting rooms that have a window opening to a garden or a vista. I can sit in front of one of his paintings and feel the pleasure and delight of his colors: his warm

Bonnard's ability to balance warm and cool colors in his palette has influenced my work and how I put colors together on the canvas. I call this painting Flowers Along the Fence.

interiors of gold and mauves and his cool exteriors of greens and blues. I love his awareness of close changes of color within the light.

His work has influenced my painting style from time to time, and I am full of joy watching the colors dance together as I put them on canvas. I have not made a garment with his palette as of yet, but it is on my mind and on my list of things to do—someday.

How would I design something when looking at one of his paintings? I'd want to embrace his sense of colors that go together and allow that palette to come alive in my knitting. I'd probably want a simple pattern with some texture in the stitches but not too much surface business, letting the changing colors do the work. Bonnard once said, "I realized that color could express everything . . . I understood that it was possible to translate light, shapes and character by color alone without the need of values." (Watkins, p. 25)

Monet

Monet's compositions are often so complex that it may be difficult to conceive how they could inspire a knitted garment. I simply take the colors I see and find my own composition in the knitted stitches. I enjoy encountering Monet's many canvases of water lilies, the study of the familiar subject within the changes of light and time of day that each canvas shares and brings to life. The uniqueness of each arrangement of color is so completely explored in his series of haystacks, poplars, and water lilies that it gives us an opportunity to notice color through a master's eyes.

I love Monet's use of yellow, so underused by many artists; it just pops out in his paintings. His brushstrokes resemble a knitted stitch as they dance across the canvas, like the ripples in the water surface. How can I take the movement of those strokes and transfer them into a knitted piece?

Monet worked *en plein air*, outdoors, often doing several paintings at a time and moving from

Monet's water lily series gave me the opportunity to use his color sense in a knitted garment.

Represent nature when it is beautiful. Everything has its moment of beauty. Beauty is the satisfaction of sight. Sight is satisfied by simplicity and order. Simplicity and order are produced in legible divisions of surface, the groupings of sympathetic colors, etc.

Quoted in Nicholas Watkins, Bonnard, p. 189

canvas to canvas as the light changed. Water lilies at twilight, with oranges, yellows, blues showing a depth in the water and a reflection of the light on the surface. *Morning*, a painting in the water lilies series, brings blues and greens, with a sliver of light reflected in gray mist. Each painting in the water lily in the series gives me a fresh look at color and light and the play of light from moment to moment. I delight in his ability to reproduce the ardent colors of a sunset and the gray mist at dawn.

Monet is the master of *plein air* painting, and he faithfully captured in his canvases the colors surrounding him outdoors. I simply enjoy his colors; they make me happy.

Paul Klee

In one of my Klee art books, I have put index cards noting "purse," "pillow," or "kid's sweater" between the pages. These markers represent the informal beginnings of new designs. In the late 1980s, using my newly acquired craft of dyeing wool, I based my first artist-inspired design on Klee's *Arab Song*.

I am constantly reminded of Klee's linear compositions, his studies of ancient calligraphy, and his love of shapes: triangles, circles, squares, and rectangles are layered into his works, and he often uses blocks of colors to play with a composition of complementary hues.

Many of his paintings seem playful to me, almost childlike, and I can visualize his colors and designs in a blanket or a wall hanging for a child's room. I find Klee's paintings lively, yet what I notice most is his palette, his own mix of unusual colors—often subtle and earthy—that work together.

Klee's Individualized Measurement of Strata *inspired this wonderful flow of color on color.*

I have already made Klee's *Individualized Measurement of Strata* as a sweater and as a pattern in my shop. I first used the colors of his original palette, then made my own color choices for the next sweater. The horizontal blocks of color made it easy to adapt elements from this painting to a knitted garment, and my knitter's stash of yarn added its own textures and colors to the composition.

Several more of his paintings will at some time become works of knitted art. *Eros* has a complexity of layers that also works with values of complementary colors imposed on a triangle for unification. The movement in *Rhythmical*, with its black, gray, and white contrasts, would make a great sitting pillow. It could be fun to work texturally with each color value—three tones, each as a different stitch—to show the rhythm of the entire piece.

So, look at Klee's work and see what you think.

> *"Paintings look at us," but in their expression, "the artist is watching us."*
>
> Quoted in Constance Naubert-Riser, *Klee: The Masterworks,* p.35.

Matisse's palette brings life to his canvas with happy colors. I love to dye these vibrant hues.

Matisse

Looking at a Matisse painting, I can tell right away that this artist loved color. His use of complementary colors, especially the vibrant green-red combination, makes his work so refreshing. His use of blue, thousands of shades of blue, astounds me. The colors keep each other happy on the canvas and therefore pleasurable to view over long periods of time. He often worked wet-on-wet, mixing colors on the canvas to make new colors.

Matisse once said, "So liberty is really the impossibility of following the path which everyone usually takes and following the one which your talents make you take." (Tériade, p. 28.) His color palette, reconstructed in colors on a simple knitted garment, would be wonderful. I am not sure how I would translate his work into a knitted piece; I might be satisfied focusing on his color interactions and go from there.

He asked in an interview, "What do I want?" In my mind, that question really is an invitation to focus and find clarity—in our lives and as artists.

Children's Artwork

Have you ever noticed how young children put colors together? Often their colors make a statement because they are bold, abstract, and full of life. Kids' artwork can grab your attention because these young artists don't follow any rules—they just apply color to paper. They do not judge their work. Provided with some paper, paints, or crayons, kids can lure us once again into the world of color.

I have often used my children's artwork to inspire a design or a palette of colors to dye on a skein. I keep many of my children's paintings in my dye studio, as a reminder that their creative eyes are a constant wonder in my life: Robin's bold red poppy, Georgia O'Keefe style; Eric's happy clown of white paint on a dark background; Dylan's trees of blue; and Emily's colorful star. Each is a beautiful, unique, and spontaneous work of art. Enjoy the art work that surrounds you, and look for the unusual colors and designs that youngsters can create.

Daughter Robin painted this red poppy while in high school, and it shows her love of color and design, inspired by Georgia O'Keefe. (above right)

Daughter Emily used crayons to draw this happy star when she was quite young. (right)

Son Eric was in grammar school and wanted to try mixed media in this painting of stark contrasts. (below right)

Son Dylan enjoyed his fantasy world as he painted trees and clouds of many colors. (below left)

The search for color did not come to me from studying paintings, but from the outside— that is, from the revelation of light in nature.

Quoted in E. Tériade, "Matisse Speaks," p. 28

Textiles

Rich greens, blues, and reds are meticulously knotted in intricate border and center medallion designs on Oriental rugs. The wool in these masterworks is all hand-dyed using natural vegetable dyes such as madder and indigo, cochineal (a dye made from small insects), and a variety of mordants such as camel urine to set the dyes. Studying the antique rugs at the Salt Bay Trading Company, where my friend David sells Kilims and fine Orientals, I wonder how the nomadic rug makers of past eras achieved such intense colors. The richness of the reds fascinates me when I think of how that color was dyed using natural materials as these people moved from place to place, gathering dyestuffs as they went.

Many of the newer rugs are made at the Tibetan Weaving Project in Nepal, using revived methods from ancient days: the wool is hand shorn and carded, spun on a drop spindle, naturally dyed, and then knotted into fine rugs. (Duplicating the colors made by natural dyestuffs can be done successfully with WashFast acid dyes by adding a speck of black to soften the color and add depth to the hues.)

Looking at the rugs from a distance gives me a sense of the whole design. I'm fascinated by the technique. With the help of a small paper pattern the rugmakers work many thousands of knots onto the warp. I look carefully at the details of color and design, appreciating the border of continuous pattern as yet another design source for a knitted fabric. Celebrate the art of these rugs—examine the ones in your house, should you be so fortunate as to own any, or visit them at a nearby rug dealer. The many books about Oriental rugs also can be good resources for color and design inspiration.

Other kinds of woven rugs can show you a new world of interesting color combinations as well. I have often focused on the incredible designs from the Bauhaus movement in Germany, noting how the artists linked color and design.

Also take a look at hooked rugs and their many shades of color, often dyed by the rug hooker. Braided and rag rugs offer their own special textures and proportions as well.

Needlepoint tapestry, in pillows or wall hangings, can be a source for knitting designs. The grid is already in place and can be transferred easily onto a knitting graph. The colors can be traditional—giving the design work a place to shine—or modern, with a new freshness for the eye to see.

Designs from fabrics such as your curtains, dishcloths, bedspreads, sofa, and clothing can often find a way into a knitted piece. I love the purity of a woven silk fabric, with its simplicity, depth of color, and texture.

I have even used Turkish socks as a source of inspiration for many designs. A friend of mine travels in Turkey and brings home these intricate hand-knit items to sell. The hand-spun wool is often rough and scratchy, yet so appealing when made into socks. The design work is amazing. These patterns, along with the wonderful color work, can easily be transferred to become a pillow or garment. Graphs of Turkish patterns are beautifully displayed in Anna Zilboorg's *Simply Socks* (see Bibliography).

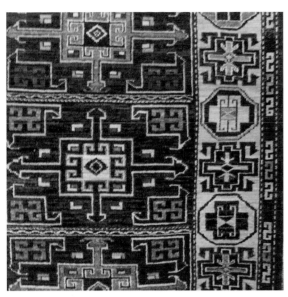

The many intricate designs of an Oriental rug can pull at you until they find their way into a knitting project some day.

I have a collection of these finely knit socks from Turkey; I wear some and keep the rest for endless ideas for patterns.

One of the best ways to see the world of color and design is through the indigenous textiles of various cultures. Look for examples from Mexico, Turkey, or African countries. Almost all regions of the globe have a textile tradition, and many interesting books have been written about them.

The blankets, sashes, footwear, and clothing of Native Americans are another window through which we can see how a people perceive the world around us. The designs and colors are rich with symbolism that is woven into the daily lives of the Hopi and the Navajo. A triangle represents a mountain; the color red is sacred and represents life. While looking at these textiles, we become aware not only of the skills involved in making these fabrics but also of the integration of beauty, ritual, and nature's resources into daily life.

I could go on and on about where we can look for inspiration, but I stress the operative word *see*. The wonderful world of color and design is easy to enter and is so rewarding.

5

the Patterns

projects for your hand-dyed yarn

Knitting is a way to balance yourself in everyday life. It is calming, enjoyable, creative, spontaneous, and grounding. Take a half-hour vacation every day. If family is at home, ask for a few undisturbed moments to knit. Do not compromise; take some time.

Find a chair, your favorite. Clean around it by getting rid of things nearby you don't want or need to see. Leave the clutter behind.

What is outside? Is it day or night, light or dark? Experience the time of day and relax into it. Take off your shoes and go barefoot.

Allow yourself to settle down and relax. Put on some music—not a news program or the television. Take a walk around your room with your eyes. What do you focus on, a flower or the colors in a painting? Sit. Breathe. Let go.

Your ability to relax before or after your day will reflect how your day is going and how you might react to a given situation at any time. Are you feeling stressed? Then knit something easy. Do you want a challenge ? Seek a complicated color chart or a new lace design. Look at a book for colorful inspiration. In this chapter I have included some of my favorite patterns, both relaxing and challenging, for you to try.

With your feet up, a quiet atmosphere surrounding you, fill your hands with fiber and start knitting. Feel the sensation and allow it to fill you. "Let your giving inspire your receiving. Realize that we cannot truly give without receiving." (Sark, *Succulent Wild Woman*, p. 173.)

A NOTE ABOUT THE PATTERNS

My philosophy is to love every stitch I am knitting; therefore the beautiful yarns used in my patterns are essential to the look of the garment. The patterns included here list specific types of yarn because they add the right touch to that particular garment. You'll find patterns that use each of the hand-dyed yarns covered in the Dyeing Procedures chapter: solid color, space-dyed, and hand-painted.

Each pattern has been tested many times by all kinds of knitters using various yarns, and each time the final project has come out a little different. We all knit in our own style, and every batch of hand-dyed yarn is unique, so no two garments *could* be exactly the same. Nonetheless, we want to end up with a finished product that fits beautifully and looks something like what we see in the published pattern, so while I encourage you to take the instructions on these patterns with a grain of salt, like a recipe that can be altered at the chef's whim, it *is* important to pay attention to certain things. First, you'll need to find and dye the perfect yarn. Visit your favorite yarn shop or check out the suppliers listed on page 126. Then, remember to *take the gauge seriously*. Check it before you start. Finally, begin your project with ease and joyful anticipation.

I am not listing substitute yarns. If you did not dye your own skeins for a particular project, there are many other wonderful yarns you can use. Look in your stash for yarns that can be used in many of the multicolored patterns. If need be, go to your favorite yarn store and pick out more textures and colors to complcte thc project.

Although I list the total amount of yarn needed in the multicolored projects, I do not give specific amounts for each separate texture or color; this is an individual decision. As you work, you may find that some yarns want to be added more, and others used less frequently. This is all part of the process of knitting—an on-the-fly decision made easily by some knitters and painfully by others.

I know the patterns work using the yarns I've specified—solid color, space-dyed, hand-painted, textured—but as far as I am concerned, any of these patterns can be tried with a different choice. Just remember that space-dyed yarn will create different effects than hand-painted yarn, so do some experimenting first. The outcome will be different if you don't use the same yarn I did, but you can take any journey as long as you are ready to rip it out if it doesn't work for you.

I believe in simplicity. These instructions are easy to follow, and when you put down your knitting, you will usually know where you are when you pick it up again. My patterns often use circular needles, which I like for several reasons. For one thing, I usually have so many colors changing from row to row that it would be difficult to match front and back if they were knitted separately—and who wants to pay that close attention? Also, I hate finishing, and with circular needles there is little sewing-up to do. Finally, many people prefer to knit rather than purl, and you always have the right side facing you.

Again, I want to stress that these patterns can be followed just as written or used as a starting point for your own creative variations. I have seen what knitters can do to individualize a pattern, and I encourage you to do this, too—change the yarn, texture, gauge, or size.

Any staff member at Pine Tree Yarns, my shop, will help you with your project (see Sources page 126). If you are involved in a knitting guild or class, share your ideas with the group. Finally, your local yarn store can help you with selecting yarns and needles and confirming your gauge.

■ EMILY'S BABY SWEATER

An easy project for a first-time mother. The body and yoke are knit in the round; sleeves are worked flat, then sewn together.

MATERIALS AND NEEDLES

1 skein dyed sport weight yarn: 4 oz (114g), 350 yds (382m)

16'' (40cm) circular needles, sizes 5 & 7 (3.75mm & 4.5mm; Can/UK sizes 9 & 7)

Single-point needles, sizes 5 & 7 (3.75mm & 4.5mm; Can/UK sizes 9 & 7)

Crochet hook

1 button

GAUGE: 20 stitches = 4'' (10cm) on size 7 (4.5mm) needles, or size needed to match gauge

FINISHED CHEST MEASUREMENT: 20'' (51cm)

WORK INSTRUCTIONS

Body

With smaller circular needle, cast on 100 stitches and place marker. Join round, being careful not to twist the stitches. K2P2 for 10 rounds. Change to larger circular needle and knit in stockinette stitch until body measures 8'' (20.5cm). At the beginning of the next round, bind off 3 stitches for underarm, knit 47 stitches, bind off 3 stitches, and knit 47 stitches. Leave work on needle.

Sleeves

With smaller straight needles, cast on 32 stitches. K2P2 for 10 rows. Change to larger needles and increase 3 stitches evenly across row. Work in stockinette stitch, increasing 1 stitch each edge every inch (2.5cm), 2 times (39 stitches total). Knit even until sleeve measures 7½'' (19cm). Bind off 2 stitches at beginning of next 2 rows (35 stitches remaining).

Yoke

Knit 35 stitches of one sleeve onto round needle, place marker, knit across 47 stitches of front, place marker, knit 2nd sleeve onto needle, place marker, knit back stitches, place marker (164 stitches total).

ROUND 1: *K1, slip 1, K1, psso (pass slipped stitch over), K to 3 stitches before marker, K2 together, K1; slip marker and repeat from * 3 more times (8 stitches decreased).

ROUND 2: Knit.

Repeat these 2 rounds 2 more times (140 stitches remain). Knit 4 rounds.

Work Pattern on next 5 rounds.

This pattern works well with variegated yarns as well as solid color.

Pattern for Yoke

ROUNDS 1 & 5: Purl.

ROUNDS 2 & 4: Knit.

ROUND 3: K2 together, YO (yarn over); repeat to end.

Knit 3 rounds. Work Pattern on next 5 rounds. Knit 1 round.

FIRST DECREASE ROUND: K2, K2 together; repeat to end (105 stitches remain). Knit 1 round.

Work third band of pattern on next 5 rounds (on Round 3: *K2 together, YO, repeat from * to end, K1). Knit 1 round.

SECOND DECREASE ROUND: K2, K2 tog; repeat to end.

At first sleeve marker, begin neck opening by working back and forth, not knitting in rounds. Knit 1 row, purl 1 row for 4 rows.

THIRD DECREASE ROW: K2, K2 together across row.

Neck ribbing: K2P2 for 4 rows. Bind off loosely.

Finishing

Sew sleeve seam and underarm. Work a row of single crochet around neck opening and crochet loop for buttonhole. Sew on button.

Knitter's Comment:

As a first-time grandmother of a darling little girl, I have a special love of knitting baby things. This little sweater was a delight and easy to do. I'd never knit on circular needles, but I am now a convert. They are quick and wonderfully easy to use. When finished, we tried the sweater on Micah. At six months it fit her nicely, with a little room to grow. If you're knitting this for an older baby, you will need to make adjustments.

—Karen Bragg

Elaine's Comment:

Emily's Baby Sweater is a great project for a new mother. The yarn is easily dyed and then easily knit on a circular needle. I like using the solid-dyed yarn, but it could be made in hand-painted yarn or space-dyed yarn for a different look. Emily is now twenty-one and was the model for the photos for this book. I love making this sweater and have knit it over and over again.

■ RIB AND GARTER STITCH SCARF

A scarf is a great way to showcase a beautiful yarn. The pattern of alternating rib and garter stitch creates a nice "woven" texture and an attractive scalloped edge.

MATERIALS AND NEEDLES

  1 skein dyed Texas (mohair/wool blend)
    sport weight, 8 oz (227g), 500 yds (456m)
  Single-point needles, size 7 (4.5mm;
    Can/UK size 7) or size needed to match gauge
  Crochet hook
GAUGE: 24 stitches = 4'' (10cm)

WORK INSTRUCTIONS

Cast on 42 stitches. Work pattern as follows until scarf measures 60'' (152cm) or desired length. If you want to add fringe, set aside 40 yards (37m) of yarn before you start the project.

Pattern

  ROW 1: Knit 7 stitches, place marker, K1P1 (rib) for 7 stitches, place marker, repeat to end of row.

  ROW 2: P1K1 (rib) 7 stitches, knit 7 stitches, repeat to end of row.

  Repeat these 2 rows 3 more times.

  ROW 9: K1P1 (rib) 7, knit 7, repeat to end of row.

  ROW 10: Knit 7, P1K1 (rib) 7, Knit 7.

  Repeat these 2 rows 3 more times.

Continue this 16-row pattern for desired length of scarf and bind off all stitches.

Knotted Fringe

Cut 96 strands of yarn that are twice the desired length of the fringe plus 1'' (2.5cm) for knotting. Pair them up to make double strands and fold each pair in half (you'll have 48 double strands).

At the first stitch on one end of scarf, use a crochet hook to pull one pair of strands through the knitted stitch so that a 1'' (2.5cm) loop projects. Slide the ends of the strands through the loop and pull tight. Continue across both ends of the scarf, spacing 24 double strands across each end.

Trim the ends of the fringe to even it up.

■ ROTHKO PULLOVER

A functional pullover with great colors

MATERIALS AND NEEDLES

Dyed worsted weight yarn in 3 colors,
   each skein 4 oz (114g), 250 yds (230m)
   Colors A & C: one skein each
   Color B: 3 (4, 4) skeins
36'' (90cm) circular needles, sizes 6 & 8
   (4mm & 5mm; Can/UK sizes 8 & 6)
16'' (40cm) circular needle, size 6
   (4mm; Can/UK size 8)
Single-point needles, sizes 6 & 8
   (4mm & 5mm; Can/UK sizes 8 & 6)
GAUGE: 16 stitches = 4'' (10cm) on size 8 needles
(5mm; Can/UK size 6) or size needed to match
gauge

FINISHED CHEST MEASUREMENTS: 44 (46, 48)''
[112 (117, 122)cm]

WORK INSTRUCTIONS

With smaller 36'' (91cm) circular needle and color
B, cast on 176 (184, 192) stitches. Join round, being
careful not to twist stitches. Place marker at beginning of round. Work in K1P1 ribbing for 4 rows.

Change to color A and continue in ribbing until
piece measures 2'' (5cm). Change to larger 36''
(90cm) circular needle and continue working with
color A in stockinette stitch until body measures 6
(7, 8)'' [15 (18, 20)cm].

Knit 2 rows with Color C.

Change to Color B and work until piece measures
16 (17, 18)'' [40.5 (43, 45.5)cm].

Divide for Front and Back

Work 82 (86, 90) stitches for back, bind off 6
stitches for underarm, work 82 (86, 90) stitches for
front, bind off 6 stitches. Put front stitches on a
holder.

Back

Working back and forth, continue in stockinette
stitch, decreasing 1 stitch each armhole edge every
4th row, 3 times, until 76 (80, 84) stitches remain.

When armhole measures 6'' (15cm) work 2 rows
of Color A.

Change to Color C and continue in stockinette
stitch until armhole measures 10 (11,12)'' [25.5 (28,
30.5)cm]. Put stitches on a holder.

Front

Work same as back until armhole measures 7 (8,
9)'' [18 (20, 23)cm]. Begin neck shaping: knit 28 (30,
32) stitches, put 20 stitches on a holder, add another ball of yarn and knit to end of row. Working

both sides at the same time, decrease 1 stitch each neck edge, every other row for 5 (6,7) times. Continue in pattern until piece measures same as back. Put shoulder stitches on holders.

Sleeves

With smaller straight needles and Color B, cast on 36 (44, 46) stitches. Work in K1P1 ribbing for 4 rows.

Change to Color A and continue in ribbing until piece measures 2'' (5cm). Change to larger needles and continue working in Color A, increasing 6 stitches evenly across next row. Increase 1 stitch each sleeve edge, every 3 rows until you have 80 (88, 96) stitches.

When sleeve measures 6 (6, 7)'' [15 (15, 18) cm], work 2 rows of Color C.

Change to Color B and work until piece measures 15 (15,16)'' [38 (38, 40.5) cm]. Work 2 rows of Color A.

Change to Color C, and continue until sleeve measures 20 (20, 21)'' [51 (51, 53.5)cm]. Bind off all stitches.

Finishing

Work 3-needle bind-off on shoulder seams, leaving 30 (32, 34) stitches for back of neck. With color C and 16'' (40cm) circular needle, pick up neck stitches; 12 (13, 14) stitches along left side, knit 20 stitches from front neck holder, pick up and knit 12 (13, 14) stitches along right side, and 30 (32, 34) stitches on back needle. Work in K1P1 ribbing for 4 rows.

Change to Color B and do 5 rows of ribbing. Bind off all stitches loosely. Sew sleeve seams, and sew sleeves in place.

Knitter's Comment:

At first this seemed too easy, and I was getting bored doing stockinette stitch, but when I put the different colors together, I enjoyed how it looked. The finished sweater is terrific.

—Nancy Johnson

Elaine's Comment:

Inspired by a Mark Rothko painting, this pullover can be made for, or by, a woman or a man. Using three colors of dyed yarn, the design is simple, functional, and unique. The colors in the example shown are subtle like the pines along the shore.

■ TRIANGLES PULLOVER

Lots of color changes make this child's sweater fun to knit. The example shown has 5 contrast colors; use fewer or more, as you prefer.

MATERIALS AND NEEDLES

Main color (MC): 1 skein dyed sport
weight yarn, 3 oz (86g), 185 yds (169m)
Contrast colors (CC): 5 skeins dyed sport
weight yarn, 2 oz (57g), 125 yds (114m) each
16'' & 24'' (40cm & 60cm) circular needles,
size 5 (3.75mm; Can/UK size 9)
Single-point needles, size 5 (3.75mm;
Can/UK size 9)

FINISHED CHEST MEASUREMENT: 24'' (61cm)

GAUGE: 24 stitches = 4'' (10cm) on size 5
(3.75mm; Can/UK size 9) needles, or size needed
to match gauge

WORK INSTRUCTIONS

Body

With MC and 24'' (60cm) circular needles, cast on 144 stitches and join together without twisting. Place marker at beginning of round.

Work seed stitch for 6 rounds: Round 1: K1P1; Round 2: P1K1.

Begin chart pattern and knit in rounds until body measures 8'' (20.5cm), selecting your own color scheme.

Divide for front and back: At the beginning of first one-color round, bind off 4 stitches for underarm, knit 68 stitches, bind off 4 stitches, and knit to end of round. Leave stitches on needle.

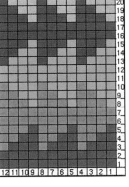

Repeat these 2 rounds twice more (200 stitches remain).

Work even for about 10 more rounds and, on a one-color round, work first decrease round as follows: K2, K2 together, repeat to end of round.

Change to 16" (40cm) circular needle and work 6 rounds, maintaining established Triangles pattern as best you can. Work second decrease round: K1, K2 together, repeat to end of round.

Work 3 rounds of solid CC. Change to MC and work 2 rounds. Do third decrease round: K2, K2 together, repeat to end of round. Work 6 rounds in seed stitch and bind off all stitches loosely.

Finishing

Sew sleeve seams and underarm opening.

Sleeves

With MC and single-point needles, cast on 34 stitches and work seed stitch for 6 rows. Increase 6 stitches evenly across next row and begin chart, changing to stockinette stitch and following color sequence as on body.

Continuing in stockinette stitch, increase 1 stitch each edge every 4th row until you have 48 stitches. Work even until sleeve measures 8" (20.5cm). Bind off 2 stitches at the beginning of the next 2 rows.

Yoke

Knit 44 stitches of one sleeve onto circular needle, place marker, knit across 68 stitches of front, place marker, knit 2nd sleeve onto circular needle, place marker, knit back stitches, place marker (224 stitches on needle). Work the following rounds as established pattern on chart. Begin yoke shaping as follows:

ROUND 1: *K1, slip 1, K1, psso, K to 3 stitches before marker, K2 together, K1, slip marker, and repeat from * 3 more times (decrease 8 stitches, 216 stitches remain).

ROUND 2: Knit, following established pattern on chart.

■ BULKY V-NECK VEST

A perfect weekend knitting project

MATERIALS AND NEEDLES

Dyed Thick-and-Thin bulky weight wool,
16 oz (454g), 245 yds (223m)
36'' (90cm) circular needle, size 15
(10mm; Can/UK 000), or size needed
to match gauge

FINISHED CHEST MEASUREMENTS: 36 (40)'' [91.5 (101.5)cm]

GAUGE: 10 stitches = 4'' (10cm)

WORK INSTRUCTIONS

Body

Cast on 92 (100) stitches and join round, being careful not to twist the stitches. Work in K2P2 ribbing for 11'' (28cm) or desired length to armhole.

DIVIDE FOR FRONT AND BACK: At beginning of next round, bind off 6 stitches for left underarm. Work in established ribbing (knit the knit stitches and purl the purl stitches) for 40 (44) stitches for the front, bind off 6 stitches for the right underarm and work 40 (44) stitches to end of the round (for the back). Put front 40 (44) stitches on a holder.

Back

Work back and forth across the 40 (44) stitches of the back in established rib pattern, decreasing 1 stitch at each armhole edge 2 times (36, 40 stitches remain). Work until armhole measures 9 (10)'' [23 (25.5)cm] or desired depth. Put all back stitches on holder or extra needle.

Skeins of thick-and-thin yarn are good candidates for solid-color dyeing. My knitter compared this bright color to golden kernels of corn.

Knitter's Comment:

This vest is a perfect weekend knitting project. The Thick-and-Thin yarn works up fast, and the ever-changing texture, coupled with Elaine's vibrant colors, make it quick, fun, and great for instant gratification. I knit it using bright gold yarn, and I think it looks like the inside of an ear of sweet yellow corn when you peel back the husk in the summer sun.

—Ellen Gilliam

Elaine's Comment:

Large needles and bulky yarn, which is easily dyed, make this a fun project for the new dyer and knitter.

Front

Pick up the 40 (44) stitches for front and work back and forth in established rib pattern, decreasing 1 stitch at each armhole edge 2 times (36, 40 stitches remain).

When front measures 2" (5cm) above beginning of arm hole, begin neck shaping.

V-NECK SHAPING: Work 16 (18) stitches, K2 together; attach another ball of yarn, K2 together, work to end of row. With 2 balls of yarn, work both sides of V-neck in established rib pattern, decreasing 1 stitch at each neck edge every other row, until 10 stitches remain for each shoulder. Work even until the fronts measure the same as the back.

Finishing

With another needle, do 3-needle bind-off at shoulders. Bind off back neck stitches. Your vest is now completed.

■ CUFF-TO-CUFF SWEATER

Delicious colors keep you intrigued while knitting

MATERIALS AND NEEDLES

6 or more skeins dyed worsted weight yarns in assorted colors, 24 oz (681g) total

36'' (90cm) circular needle, size 8 (5mm; Can/UK size 6), or size needed to match gauge

16'' (40cm) circular needle, size 6 (4 mm; Can/UK size 8)

FINISHED CHEST MEASUREMENT: 40'' (101.5cm)

GAUGE: 16 stitches = 4'' (10cm) in stockinette stitch

WORK INSTRUCTIONS

Sleeve

Cast on 40 stitches with the longer circular needle. Do NOT join round; this sweater is worked back and forth.

Work 6 ridges of garter stitch (knit every row), then begin working garter stitch and stockinette stitch pattern as follows: work random-width strips of garter stitch and stockinette stitch, changing colors with each new strip. Increase 1 stitch on each side of sleeve every 6th row, 6 times (52 stitches).

Work even until piece measures 10'' (25.5cm), then increase 1 stitch on each side every 4th row, 8 times (68 stitches).

Work even until sleeve measures 19'' (48.25cm). Measuring textured knitting might be tricky. Find a flat spot to lay down the garment so you can be sure to get an accurate measurement.

Body

When sleeve measures approximately 19'' (48.25cm), begin a new color and cast on 56 stitches at the beginning of the next 2 rows (180 stitches). Continue working pattern of garter stitch and stockinette stitch strips for 6'' (15cm).

BACK: Work 90 stitches and place them on holder. The stitches remaining on circular needle are for sweater back. Continue working in pattern, decreasing 1 stitch at neck edge one time to shape neck opening. Work back for 8'' (20cm). Add 1 stitch at neck edge of next row to shape neck opening. Put the back stitches on holder (to be joined to front later).

FRONT: Pick up stitches for front and work in color pattern to match back, shaping neck opening by decreasing 2 stitches at neck edge one time,

Sleeve detail of Cuff-to-Cuff Sweater in a rainbow colorway.

then 1 stitch at neck edge every other row 6 times (14 rows). Work even until 14 rows before end of neck opening (refer to back to count total number of rows in neck opening), then finish front neck shaping by increasing 1 stitch every other row 6 times and 2 stitches one time.

JOIN FRONT TO BACK: Continue to work in pattern for 6" (15cm). Finish body of sweater by binding off 56 stitches at the beginning of the next 2 rows (68 stitches remain).

Sleeve

Continue working on sleeve, decreasing 1 stitch each edge every 4th row 8 times, and then decreasing 1 stitch at each edge every 6 rows (40 stitches remain). When second sleeve measures the same length as first sleeve and you have worked 6 ridges of garter stitch, bind off all stitches.

Finishing

Sew side seams and sleeve seams.

NECK: With shorter circular needle, pick up stitches around neck opening. Work in garter stitch for 1" (2.5cm). Bind off stitches.

Optional Lower Edge

With longer circular needle, pick up stitches along bottom edge of sweater and work in garter stitch or K2P2 ribbing for 2" (5cm). Bind off stitches. A garter stitch edge will make the sweater more like a tunic; K2P2 ribbing will make a more fitted garment.

Knitter's Comment:

The thing is, I have a really low boredom threshold. Felicitously, Elaine does too! This Cuff-to-Cuff Sweater is perfect for knitters with undiagnosed ADD. The colors and textures change just often enough, particularly with hand-dyed yarn, to keep even my attention riveted.

—Kate Braestrup

Elaine's Comment:

I picked this pattern because it allows you to be as creative and as focused on color and texture as you want to be. This garment can have any personality—dyed in rainbow colors or in a monochrome of reds. It is easy to knit, and the flow of color changes makes you want to keep going until the last stitch. Dyeing the yarn for this project can also be an adventure!

■ CHILD'S WOVEN PULLOVER AND HAT

Space-dyed yarn adds color changes without any effort

MATERIALS AND NEEDLES

1 skein dyed sport weight yarn, 4 oz (114g), 350 yds (320m) (MC)

1 skein dyed Texas (mohair/wool blend) sport weight, 8 oz (227g), 500 yds (456 m) (CC)

Straight needles, size 6 (4mm; Can/UK size 8)

16'' (40cm) circular needle, size 6 (4mm; Can/UK size 8) for hat

Double-point needles, size 6 (4 mm; Can/UK size 8)

GAUGE: 20 stitches = 4'' (10cm) in basketweave stitch

FINISHED CHEST MEASUREMENTS:
Pullover: 24 (26, 28)'' [61 (66, 71)cm
Hat: 19'' (48cm)

WORK INSTRUCTIONS—PULLOVER

NOTE: You are making both front and back all in one piece, worked flat, and sewing up the side seam at the end.

Body

With MC, cast on 120 (132, 138) stitches and work back and forth in K1P1 ribbing for 1 (2, 2)'' [2.5 (5, 5)cm]. Begin basketweave stitch pattern as follows:

ROW 1: Knit MC.

ROW 2: Purl MC.

ROW 3: Knit 3 MC, Knit 3 CC.

ROW 4: Purl 3 MC, Knit 3 CC.

ROW 5: Knit 3 MC, Purl 3 CC.

ROW 6: Purl 3 MC, Knit 3 CC.

ROWS 7 & 8: Repeat rows 1 & 2.

ROW 9: Knit 3 CC, Knit 3 MC.

ROW 10: Knit 3 CC, Purl 3 MC.

ROW 11: Purl 3 CC, Knit 3 MC.

ROW 12: Knit 3 CC, Purl 3 MC.

Repeat these 12 rows until piece measures 7 (8, 9)'' [18 (20, 23)cm].

SHAPE ARMHOLES: At beginning of next row, bind off 3 stitches, knit in pattern for 57 (63, 66) stitches, bind off 3 stitches, and work until end of row. Put front stitches on a holder.

Back

Continue in established basketweave pattern until piece measures approximately 12 (14, 15)'' [30.5 (35.5, 38)cm] including ribbing.

TOP EDGE: After 2 rows of MC, work 2 ridges (4 rows) of garter stitch with MC. Bind off all stitches.

Front

Make the front the same as the back.

Sleeves

With MC, cast on 34 (36, 40) stitches and work in K1P1 ribbing for 1 (2, 2)'' [2.5 (5, 5)cm]. Begin Ridge pattern as follows:

ROW 1: Knit MC.

ROW 2: Purl MC.

ROW 3: Knit CC.

ROW 4: Knit CC.

ROW 5: Purl CC.

ROW 6: Knit CC.

Repeat these 6 pattern rows for rest of sleeve, increasing 1 stitch at each edge of every 4th row

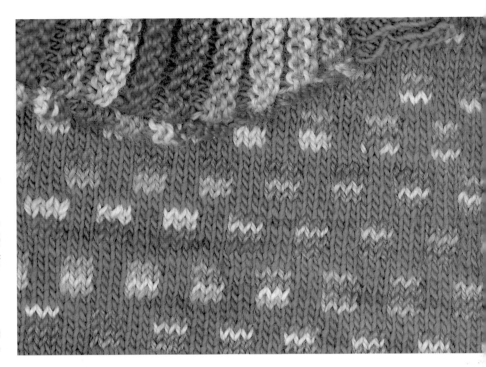

6 (7, 10) times, until there are 46 (50, 60) stitches. Continue in pattern until sleeve measures 7 (8, 10)'' [17.75 (20, 25.5)cm] or desired length. Bind off all stitches.

Finishing

Sew side seam of body from bottom edge to level of sleeve opening. Sew shoulder seams 2'' (5cm) in from each side, and that gives you the neck opening. Sew sleeve seams and sew sleeves in place.

WORK INSTRUCTIONS—HAT

Sherry Hughes came up with this little hat to complete the outfit and use up extra yarn.

With MC, cast on 96 stitches using 16'' (40cm) circular needle. Join round, being careful not to twist stitches. Place marker.

Work in Rib pattern as follows:

ROUNDS 1 & 2: Knit MC.

ROUNDS 3–6: Knit 2 CC, Purl 2 MC.

ROUNDS 7 & 8: Knit 2, Purl 2 in MC.

ROUNDS 9–12: Knit 2 MC, Purl 2 CC.

Work Ridge pattern as follows:

ROUNDS 1 & 2: Knit MC.

ROUND 3: Knit CC.

ROUNDS 4–6: Purl CC.

Repeat these 6 rounds 5 times.

With MC, knit 1 round. Begin decrease rounds:

ROUND 1: Knit 22 stitches, K2 together, repeat 5 times. Change to double-point needles.

ROUND 2: Knit 21 stitches, K2 together; repeat to end.

Continue to decrease every round until 8 stitches remain. Break yarn, and with yarn needle run tail through these stitches, draw them together, and fasten securely.

Knitter's Comment:

Knitting with Elaine's vibrant yarn brightened my attitude! The colors are so uplifting.

—Sherry Hughes

Elaine's Comment:

Dyed yarn and luscious space-dyed mohair/wool blend make this a wonderful project, especially if you have dyed the yarn yourself. You can see how interestingly space-dyed yarn can knit up in its own unique patterns—and look good in the design of a garment. I wanted the textured stitch pattern and the space-dyed yarn to each make a design on its own.

■ WOVEN PULLOVER AND HAT

Elegant and easy to make.

MATERIALS AND NEEDLES

Contrast color (CC): 2 skeins dyed Texas (mohair/wool blend) sport weight, 8 oz (227g), 500 yds (456m) each

Main color (MC): 2 (3) skeins dyed sport weight yarn, 4 oz (114g), 350 yds (320m) each

36'' (90cm) circular needle, sizes 5 & 7 (3.75mm & 4.5mm; Can/UK sizes 9 & 7)

Straight needles, sizes 5 & 7 (3.75mm & 4.5mm; Can/UK sizes 9 & 7)

16'' (40cm) circular needle, sizes 5 & 6 (3.75mm & 4mm; Can/UK sizes 9 & 8)

GAUGE: In basketweave stitch, 26 stitches = 4'' (10cm) on size 7 (4.5mm) needles, or size needed to match gauge.

FINISHED CHEST SIZES: 38 (42)'' [96.5 (107)cm]

WORK INSTRUCTIONS—PULLOVER

Body

With MC and smaller 36'' (90cm) circular needle, cast on 246 (276) stitches. Join round, being careful not to twist stitches. Place marker.

BEGIN 2-COLOR RIBBING: Purl 1 MC, Knit 2 CC. Work for 2½" (5cm).

Change to larger circular needle and start basketweave stitch pattern as follows:

ROWS 1 & 2: Knit MC.

ROW 3: Knit 3 MC, Knit 3 CC.

ROWS 4–6: Knit 3 MC, Purl 3 CC.

ROWS 7 & 8: Knit MC.

ROW 9: Knit 3 CC, Knit 3 MC.

ROWS 10–12: Purl 3 CC, Knit 3 MC.

Repeat these 12 rows until piece measures 14" (35.5cm) or desired length to armhole.

DIVIDE FOR FRONT AND BACK: At marker, bind off 6 stitches, continue in pattern for 117 (132) stitches, bind off 6 stitches for second armhole, and continue in pattern for 117 (132) stitches. Put front stitches on holder.

Back

Work back and forth in established pattern, changing the stitches on wrong side of work now that you are no longer working in the round (for example, row 2 becomes a purl row). Work until armhole measures 8½" (21.5cm).

Neck shaping: Work 42 (49) stitches, put 33 (34) stitches on holder, add additional balls of yarn, work 42 (49) stitches. Keeping in pattern, decrease 1 stitch at each neck edge 4 times. Work for 1½" (3.75cm). Put shoulder stitches on holders.

Front:

Pick up front stitches and work as instructed for back.

Sleeves

Using smaller size straight needles, cast on 51 stitches with MC. Work patterned rib for 2" (5cm): Purl 1 MC, Knit 2 CC.

Change to larger straight needles and with MC knit 1 row, increasing 20 stitches evenly across row. Purl 1 row. Start pattern as follows:

ROW 1: Knit MC.

ROW 2: Purl MC.

ROWS 3–6: Knit CC.

Repeat these 6 rows for garter rib stitch. Increase 1 stitch at each edge every 10th row until there are 94 stitches. Work in pattern until there are 26 garter ridges. Bind off all stitches.

Finishing

Do a 3-needle bind off at shoulder seams.

With size 5 (3.75mm; Can/UK size 9) 16'' (40cm) circular needle, pick up neck stitches from front holder, along side of neck, and from on back holder (99 stitches total). Knit 2 CC, Purl 1 MC as in ribbing for 2'' (5 cm). Bind off all stitches in MC.

Sew sleeve seams; sew sleeves to underarm.

WORK INSTRUCTIONS—HAT

Using 16'' (40cm) circular needle, size 6 (4mm; Can/UK8), cast on 110 stitches with MC. Join round, being careful not to twist stitches. Place marker. Work in rib pattern as follows:

Rib Pattern

ROUNDS 1 & 2: Knit MC.

ROUNDS 3–8: Knit 2 CC, Purl 2 MC.

ROUNDS 9 & 10: Knit 2, Purl 2 in MC.

ROUNDS 11–16: Knit 2 MC, Purl 2 CC.

Knit one round using MC only, increasing 10 stitches evenly across round (120 stitches). Begin ridge pattern in next round.

Ridge Pattern

ROUNDS 1 & 2: Knit MC.

ROUND 3: Knit CC.

ROUNDS 4–6: Purl CC.

Repeat these 6 rounds 6 times.

Shape Crown

With MC, knit 2 rounds. Begin decrease rounds:

ROUND 1: Knit 22 stitches, K2 together, repeat to end of round. Change to double-point needles.

ROUND 2: Knit 21 stitches, K2 together; repeat to end.

Continue to decrease every round until 8 stitches remain. Break yarn and with yarn needle run tail through these stitches, drawing them together. Fasten securely.

___

Knitter's Comment:

I would like to impart two observations about knitting with space-dyed yarn. First, it adds great inspiration and stimulation to the craft of knitting—in itself a rewarding and creative pastime. The vibrancy of Elaine's dyeing calls out to you to be lighthearted and innovative, even daring in your efforts. The results never seem to disappoint. Second, more contemplative in scope: knitting with space-dyed yarn carries you on a bit of a journey—one shade connecting with the next, the colors surprisingly harmonious and interconnected, dependent on each other for a successful result— a lesson in diversity and tolerance, the tangible product more powerful for the blending.

—Kathleen Kennedy

Elaine's Comment:

I made the pattern for the Child's Woven Pullover first, and my customers wanted to make it for themselves, so I made an adult pattern as well. I adapted Sherry Hughes's pattern for little matching child's hat to adult size as well. Using space-dyed yarn in this pattern is very satisfying because the color changes happen by magic as you are knitting.

■ BASIC BERET

A wonderful beret for any outing

MATERIALS AND NEEDLES

1 skein space-dyed worsted weight yarn,
4 oz (114g), 250 yds (229m)

16'' (40cm) circular needle, size 9
(5.5mm; Can/UK size 5)

Double-point needles, size 9
(5.5mm; Can/UK size 5)

FINISHED MEASUREMENT: 22'' (56cm)

GAUGE: 13 stitches = 4'' (10cm)

WORK INSTRUCTIONS

Using circular needle, cast on 76 stitches. Join round, being careful not to twist stitches. Work K1P1 ribbing for 1'' (2.5cm). Put marker at beginning of next round.

FIRST INCREASE ROUND: Knit 2, increase 1 in next stitch; repeat 25 times, end knit 1 (101 stitches total).

Knit one round.

NEXT INCREASE ROUND: Knit 7, increase 1 in next stitch; repeat 11 times (112 stitches).

Knit even until piece measures approximately 6'' (15cm).

Top Shaping

ROUND 1: Knit 12, K2 together, 8 times (104 stitches).

ROUNDS 2 & 4: Work even.

ROUND 3: Knit 11, K2 together, 8 times.

Continue to decrease 8 stitches every other round, as above, having one less stitch between decreases on each decrease round. When 64 stitches

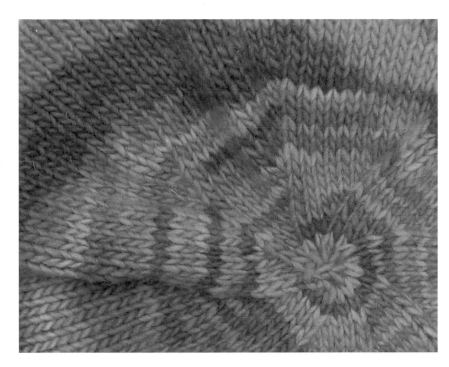

remain, change to double-point needles and decrease stitches every round until 8 stitches remain.

Finishing

Break off yarn and, with a yarn needle, run tail through these stitches and draw stitches together. Fasten securely. Wash beret and block flat.

Knitter's Comment:

I was given this space-dyed yarn and asked to make a beret. I usually make scarves, so this was a challenge. Once I got started, I was fascinated by how the colors made their own design as I was knitting. This was a fun project for a new knitter like me.

—Emily Davey

■ TEXTURED SCARF

Space-dyed yarn and texture make this scarf beautiful

MATERIALS AND NEEDLES

1 skein space-dyed Texas (wool/mohair blend) yarn, 8 oz (227g), 500 yds (456m)

Size 7 (4.5mm; Can/UK size 7) single-point needles, or size needed to match gauge

Assorted yarns for fringe

FINISHED MEASUREMENTS: 9'' x 60'' (23cm x 152cm)

GAUGE: 18 stitches = 4'' (10cm)

WORK INSTRUCTIONS

Cast on 41 stitches. Work 6 rows of seed stitch as follows: Slip 1, *K1, P1, repeat from * to end of row.

Begin Textured Stitch pattern:

ROWS 1 & 3: Slip 1, K1, P1, K1; Knit to last 4 stitches, K1, P1, K2.

ROW 2: Slip 1, K1, P1, K1; *K1, P1, repeat from * to last 4 stitches; K1, P1, K2.

ROW 4: Slip 1, K1, P1, K1; *P1, K1, repeat from * to last 4 stitches; K1, P1, K2.

Repeat these 4 rows until scarf measures 60'' (152cm) or desired length. Work 6 rows of seed stitch. Bind off all stitches.

Block with damp cloth if needed.

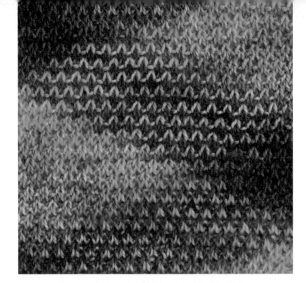

Knitter's Comment:

I love scarves! I love to make them, and I love to wear them. If you feel the same way, you definitely need to try this yarn and this pattern. The yarn is a mohair blend. It is so soft that it feels like it must contain silk. Space-dyed yarn, in this stitch pattern, just dances back and forth across the scarf. I discovered two things using this yarn and pattern. First, you must keep the stitches snug and stay up on the ends of your needles. Second, if you have a strong color contrast in your yarn, you will see more color movement and the texture of the stitches will be less noticeable. However, if you have a more subtle color variation in your yarn, your stitch pattern will be more pronounced. Either way, I think you will be delighted with this project. It performs beautifully in color and in texture providing a unique abundance of possibilities. Knit on!

—Cindy Flood

Knotted Fringe

Using yarns of several different textures, cut 92 strands of yarn that are twice the desired length of the fringe plus 1" (2.5cm) for knotting. Pair them up to make double strands and fold each pair in half (you'll have 46 double strands).

At the first stitch on one end of scarf, use a crochet hook to pull one pair of strands through the knitted stitch so that a 1" (2.5cm) loop projects. Slide the ends of the strands through the loop and pull tight. Continue across both ends of the scarf, spacing 22 double strands across each end.

Trim the ends of the fringe to even it up.

Elaine's Comment:

A beautiful space-dyed yarn and a nice easy pattern give this scarf the appearance of being difficult to knit. In fact, it is an easy project that flows with a zigzag color sequence that is pleasing to create. The yarn does the work for you, just knit it!

■ TEE-SHIRT

Color and texture are key to this tee, in which the sleeves are worked together with the body pieces.

MATERIALS AND NEEDLES

Color A: 1 skein space-dyed Mikado bulky weight, 8 oz (227g), 155 yds (142m)

Color B: 1 skein hand-painted Thick-and-Thin wool, 16 oz (454g), 245 yds (228m)

Colors C and D: 2 skeins Brown Sheep Company worsted weight, 4 oz (114g), 190 yds (174m) each

29'' (74cm) circular needles, sizes 9 & 10½ (5.5mm and 6.5mm; Can/UK sizes 5 and 3)

GAUGE: 14 stitches = 4'' (72cm) on 10½ (6.5mm; Can/UK size 3) needles, or size needed to match gauge

FINISHED CHEST MEASUREMENT: 42'' (107cm)

WORK INSTRUCTIONS

Back

Using smaller circular needle, cast on 72 stitches with Color D. Do not join round; sweater is worked back and forth in rows. Work garter ribbing pattern as follows:

ROW 1: Knit.

ROW 2: K2P2.

Work for 6 rows. Change to larger needle.

Work 6 rows of Color A in garter ribbing, 4 rows of Color B, 2 rows of Color C/D. Continue in garter ribbing pattern, maintaining the 6, 4, 2 row repeat and alternating Colors C and D for the 2-row stripe, until piece measures 12'' (30.5cm).

Tee-Shirt Sweater in a different colorway.

Sleeves

Cast on 3 stitches at beginning of the next 4 rows, using a cable cast-on.* Cast on 10 stitches at beginning of next 2 rows using the same cast-on (104 stitches on needle).

Work for 8" (20.5cm) in established pattern.

Neck Shaping and Shoulders

Work pattern for 40 stitches, place 24 stitches on a holder for neck, work to end of row. Attaching another ball of yarn, work both shoulders at the same time. Bind off 2 stitches at each neck edge once and 1 stitch at each edge 2 times.

Put shoulder stitches on stitch holders.

Front

Work same as back until sleeves measure 6" (15.5cm), then work 4 rows of neck shaping as on back. Continue in established pattern until piece measures the same total length as back.

Finishing

Join shoulder seams using 3-needle bind-off.

NECK: With smaller circular needle pick up stitches around neck and work 4 rows of garter ribbing in Color D. Bind off all stitches.

Sew side and underarm seams.

* Insert right needle between *first 2 stitches* on left needle when making the new stitch. For a more detailed description, see The Harmony Guide to Knitting Stitches or other basic knitting manual, or a Web site such as knitting.about.com.

SLEEVE EDGING (OPTIONAL): Pick up stitches along bottom edge of sleeve and work in ribbing for 5 rows. Bind off all stitches. Enjoy your new tee-shirt!

Knitter's Comment:

The pattern is simple (basically 2 rows and 4 stitches), and it is made absolutely gorgeous by the rotation of the colors. I knit a couple of swatches to see how I liked the color distribution. It wasn't until the sweater was finished and presented to Elaine that I realized I had misinterpreted the pattern—but it's really not possible to make a mistake when working this pattern. Just make sure you have plenty of yarn. After completing this project, I dashed right to my own collection of yarn and chose 12 colors to make my version. I cannot be limited to four colors, especially after learning Elaine's philosophy, "When in doubt, add more color." This sweater is fun, easy, and quick to knit, and I'm sure you will enjoy knitting it as I did.

—Linda Murdock

Elaine's Comment:

Several textures and space-dyed yarn give this tee-shirt an interesting appearance that can have a new personality every time you knit it. A simple pattern repeat and great yarns make this a winner. You can knit this sweater over and over in all weights of yarn; just determine the new gauge and recalculate your number of stitches to fit the yarns being used.

■ GATHERED VEST

*Earthy hand-painted yarn makes this a
wonderful project.*

MATERIALS AND NEEDLES

Main color (MC): 1 skein space-dyed sport
   weight yarn, 4 oz (114g), 350 yds (320m)
Contrast colors (CC): 4 skeins hand-painted
   worsted weight yarn, 4 oz (114g), 250 yds
   (229m) each
29'' (74cm) circular needle, sizes 7 & 9
   (4.5mm & 5.5mm; Can/UK sizes 7 & 5)
16'' (40cm) circular needle, size 7
   (4.5mm; Can/UK size 7)
7 buttons, ³⁄₈'' (9mm)

FINISHED CHEST MEASUREMENTS: 38 (40)''
[96 (101)cm]

GAUGE: In garter stitch, 20 stitches = 4'' (10cm) on
size 7 (4.5mm; Can/UK size 7) needles, or size
needed to match gauge.

WORK INSTRUCTIONS

Body

   With smaller 29'' (74cm) circular needle, cast on
180 (200) stitches with MC. Do not join round; this
vest is worked back and forth.

   Work 3 rows of garter stitch (band pattern), making first buttonhole on 4th row as follows: knit 2
stitches, bind off 2 stitches; work to end of row.
Next row: Knit to bound-off stitches, cast on the 2
stitches and knit 2 stitches.

Continue working garter stitch for 3 more rows. At 10th row (wrong side facing), begin first band of gathered-stitch pattern.

GATHERED-STITCH PATTERN: Still working with MC, increase 1 stitch in each stitch across row—360 (400) stitches total. Change to larger circular needle and first CC and work 6 rows of stockinette stitch. On next row (right side facing), change back to MC and smaller needle, decrease back down to 180 (200) stitches by K2 together across row.

Work 5 rows of garter stitch with MC. On wrong side, at row 6, start gathered pattern again by increasing stitches.

Continue working the MC garter stitch bands and CC gathered-stitch bands, changing yarns and needles each time. Continue making buttonholes at every other MC band.

Glass buttons by Chris DeLisle

Divide for Front and Back

Begin armholes on 8th MC band: on 5th row of garter stitch, knit 41 (46) stitches for right front, bind off 8 stitches, knit 82 (92) stitches for back, bind off 8 stitches, knit remaining stitches for left front. Put both sets of front stitches on holders.

Back

Continue doing bands of MC garter stitch and CC gathered stitch on back until there are 14 MC bands. Bind off stitches in MC.

Front

Continue doing bands and gathers, matching CC sequence on back and working buttonholes in every other MC garter stitch band as you go.

When you have worked 2 rows on the 13th MC band, bind off 14 stitches at beginning of each neck edge. Continue working until 14 MC bands are completed. Bind off all stitches with MC.

Finishing

Sew front and back at shoulders. Pick up and knit all neck stitches with 16'' (40cm) circular needle and MC. Make last buttonhole and work 2 more rows of garter stitch for neck edging. Bind off all stitches. Sew on buttons and enjoy!!

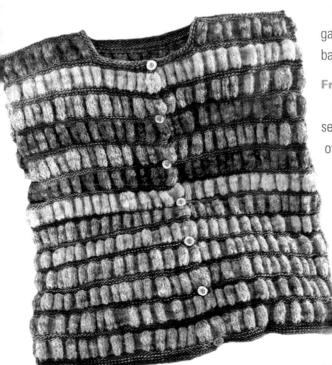

■ FLEECE-LINED MITTENS

Warm and toasty for winter activities, "stuffed" mittens became popular in this country after Robin Hansen's Fox & Geese & Fences, *a book of traditional mitten patterns, was published in 1983. The original Canadian folk mittens use bits of unspun fleece for the lining, but this pattern calls for lengths of bulky yarn instead.*

MATERIALS AND NEEDLES

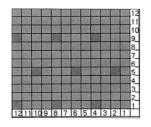

1 skein hand-painted worsted weight yarn,
   4 oz (114g), 250 yds (230m)
2 oz bulky weight yarn in a contrasting color,
   cut into 3'' (7.5cm) strips for "fleece"
Single-point needles, sizes 4 & 6 (3.5mm
   & 4mm; Can/UK sizes 9 & 8)

FINISHED SIZES: Small (age 3–6), Medium (8–teens), Large (adult)
GAUGE: 18 stitches = 4'' (10.25cm) on size 6 (4mm; Can/UK size 8) needles, or size needed to match gauge

WORK INSTRUCTIONS

Cut bulky yarn into 3'' (7.75cm) pieces to use as fleece stuffing. It is helpful to cut up plenty of fleece bits ahead of time. You will need about 100 to line a size Large mitten.

Cast on 26 (30, 34) stitches with smaller needles. Work in K1P1 ribbing for 3'' (7.75cm).

Change to larger needles and begin stockinette stitch, increasing 6 stitches evenly in the next row—32 (36, 40) stitches. Work 3 more rows.

NEXT ROW: Knit 3 stitches and add fleece beginning with the next stitch, as follows: insert right needle into stitch as if to knit and put yarn around needle as usual; now add fleece piece by looping it around the right needle and the stitch, keeping fleece ends at back of work; knit both fleece and working yarn onto needle together. (Fleece and yarn together count as 1 stitch.) Continue across the row, adding fleece at every 4th stitch.

Work 6 (8, 10) more rows, adding fleece bits on every 4th row (always a knit row) and staggering the fleece stitches from row to row as shown in chart.

Thumb Gusset

Continue inserting bits of fleece according to established pattern as you increase for the thumb gusset:

ROW 1: Knit 15 (17, 19) stitches, place marker on needle, increase 1 stitch in each of the next 2 stitches, place marker, K 15 (17, 19) stitches.

ROW 2: Purl.

ROW 3: Knit to marker, slip marker, increase in next stitch and knit to one stitch before marker, increase 1 stitch, slip marker, and knit to end of row.

Repeat rows 2 & 3 until there are 10 (12, 14) stitches between markers. Purl one row. On the next knit row, knit to 1 stitch before marker and increase in that stitch (add 1 stitch), put the 10 (12, 14) stitches between markers on holder for thumb, increase 1 stitch in next stitch, and knit to end of row.

Purl across next row, joining stitches for the hand and leaving thumb stitches on holder.

Hand

Work even, adding fleece according to established pattern, until mitten measures 8 (9, 10½)" [20.5 (23, 26.5) cm] or desired length, ending with a purl row. Start top shaping:

ROW 1: K2, K2 together, repeat to end.

ROWS 2 & 4: Purl.

ROW 3: K1, K2 together, repeat to end.

ROW 5: K2 together, repeat to end.

Cut yarn, leaving a 15" (38cm) tail. Draw tail through remaining stitches using a yarn needle, and fasten inside, sewing side seam.

Thumb

Pick up 10 (12, 14) stitches from holder and work even, adding fleece according to established pattern, until thumb measures 1½ (2, 2½)" [3 (5, 6.5) cm]. K2 together across row and finish as with hand.

Knitter's Comment:

Making mittens, for me, is like baking bread— an act of faith and love for those of us who live where the winters are cold. Try knitting these in different moods, from elegant mittens using luxurious hand-dyed yarns and soft merino or alpaca fleece, to rugged working mitts knit from sturdy wool and lightly washed fleece with a gentle scent of sheep. The pattern can also be easily adapted to four-needle knitting for seamless mittens—just divide the stitches among four needles, join, and knit!

—Lynn Plumb

Elaine's Comment:

This is a satisfying project because the colors blend into one another so nicely and the fleece adds to the pattern. Fun to make for everyone, young or old, as they take very little time.

■ SLIP STITCH VEST

Easy color changes and stitchwork make this a winner.

MATERIALS AND NEEDLES

Main color (MC): 1 skein dyed worsted weight wool, 4 oz (114g), 250 yds (230m)

Contrast colors (CC): yarns of assorted colors and textures, including one or more hand painted, worsted weight or equivalent, 22 oz (567g), 750 yds (685m) total

29" (74cm) circular needle, size 8 (5mm; Can/UK size 6) or size needed to match gauge

4 buttons, ¾" (20mm)

FINISHED CHEST MEASUREMENT: 38" (96.5cm)

GAUGE: 18 stitches = 4" (10cm)

WORK INSTRUCTIONS

Speckle Rib Pattern: multiple of 2, plus 1 stitch.

ROW 1: Knit.

ROW 2: Purl.

ROW 3: Change color. Knit 1, *slip 1 purlwise, knit 1; repeat from * to end.

ROW 4: Knit 1, *yarn forward, slip 1 purlwise, yarn back, knit 1. Repeat from * to end.

ROWS 5 & 6: Repeat rows 1 & 2.

ROW 7: Change color. Knit 2, *slip 1 purlwise, knit 1; repeat from * to end.

ROW 8: Knit 2, *yarn forward, slip 1 purlwise, yarn back, knit 1. Repeat from * to end.

Body

With MC, cast on 173 stitches. Do not join round; this vest is worked back and forth. Work K1P1 ribbing for 6 rows.

Begin Speckle Rib stitch pattern and work until piece measures 13" (33cm) or desired length to

The Slip Stitch pattern is a good way to use many solid and variegated dyed yarns together.

armhole, changing colors and textures as desired at the beginning of rows 3 and 7 of pattern.

Divide for front and back: Work pattern for 38 stitches, bind off 10 stitches for underarm and work to end of row. Next row, work 38 stitches, bind off 10 stitches. Put front stitches on holders.

Back

Armhole edging: Knit first 6 stitches of every row for garter stitch band along armhole.

Continue in established pattern, working garter stitch band and decreasing 1 stitch at armhole edges every other row 2 times, then work straight until piece measures 9'' (23cm) above beginning of armhole.

Shape back neck: K 22 stitches, bind off 28 stitches, knit to end of row. Put shoulder stitches on holders.

Fronts

Pick up front stitches and continue in established pattern, working garter stitch band as for back and decreasing 1 stitch at armhole edge every other row 2 times. Shape front neck by decreasing 1 stitch at neck edge every other row until 22 stitches

remain (including armhole band stitches). Work until front piece measures same as back.

Finishing

Join shoulders using 3-needle bind-off.

Neck and front edging: With MC, pick up stitches along one front edge, across back neck, and along edge of other front piece. K1P1 for 2 rows. On 3rd row, begin working buttonholes: K1P1 for 4 stitches, bind off 2 stitches, *K1P1 for 10 stitches and bind off 2 stitches for buttonhole. Repeat from * 2 more times (4 buttonholes total) and work to end of row. Next row: cast on 2 stitches over bound-off stitches. Work 2 more rows. Bind off loosely in K1P1 rib.

Sew on buttons.

Knitter's Comment:

When Elaine first gave me the yarn for this vest, I was surprised that so many colors, weights, and textures would be used. She told me to just pick up a skein and go, with no particular color sequence. I was accustomed to a more structured use of yarn. Wary at first, I persevered, and as the project progressed, I was amazed at how the colors and textures blended so well. It was a very liberating experience.

—Yvonne Lamoreaux

Elaine's Comment:

Lots of colors and different textures make this exciting to knit. Using the hand-painted yarn and contrasting colors allows for free-flowing color combinations. Try a theme like a tide pool or the sherbet colors of summer. This is a great way to use up some of your stash if you're not in the mood to dye a lot of yarn.

■ MAINE BOUNTY SWEATER

Color and a simple pattern make a great sweater.

MATERIALS AND NEEDLES

1 skein hand-painted worsted weight yarn,
4 oz (114g), 250 yds (230m)

14 oz (397g) silk, mohair, boucle, and wool yarns
in various colors

16'' (40cm) & 35'' (89cm) circular needle,
size 5 (3.75mm; Can/UK size 9)

35'' (89cm) circular needle, size 7
(4.5mm; Can/UK size 7)

Straight needles, sizes 5 & 7 (3.75mm & 4.5mm;
Can/UK sizes 9 & 7)

GAUGE: 20 stitches = 4'' (10cm) on size 7 (4.5mm;
Can/UK size 7) needles, or size needed to match
gauge

FINISHED CHEST MEASUREMENTS: 36 (38, 40)''
[91.5 (96.5, 102)cm]

WORK INSTRUCTIONS

Body

Cast on 180 (192, 200) stitches with the smaller
35'' (89cm) circular needle. Join round, being careful not to twist stitches. K1P1 for 2'' (5cm). Change
to larger size 35'' (89cm) circular needle.

The body is worked in stockinette stitch (knit
every round), using various colors and textures for
one or two rounds at a time, changing randomly
throughout the project. To add the new color, knit 2
stitches of the old color together with the next color
so no holes or knots are made.

When body reaches 13 (14,15)'' [33 (35.5, 38)cm],
divide for front and back: knit 86 (92, 96) stitches for
back, bind off 4 stitches for underarm, knit 86 (92,

PHOTOGRAPH BY NANCE TRUEWORTHY

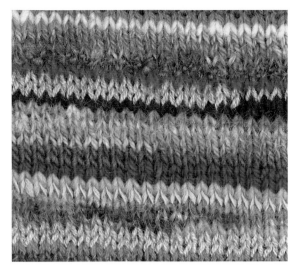

Both earthy and bright color combinations work beautifully in the Maine Bounty pattern.

96) stitches for front and bind off 4 stitches. Put front stitches on holder.

Back

Work back until armhole measures 8'' (20cm).

Neck shaping: knit 28 (31, 33) stitches, put 30 stitches on holder, add another ball of yarn and knit remaining stitches. Knit for 1'' (2.5cm) Put shoulder stitches on holders.

Front

Pick up front stitches and work as for back until armhole measures 6½'' (16.5cm).

Neck shaping: knit 31 (34, 36) stitches, put 24 stitches on holder for neck, add another ball of yarn and knit remaining stitches. Decrease one stitch at each neck edge every other row 3 times, 28 (31, 33) stitches remain. Work until front is same length as back and put shoulder stitches on holders or spare needle.

Sleeves

With smaller size straight needles, cast on 42 (44, 46) stitches and work ribbing for 2'' (5cm). Change to larger straight needles and increase 6 stitches evenly across. Increase 1 stitch at each side every inch (2.5cm) 14 times. When sleeve measures 18'' (45.5 cm) or desired length, bind off all stitches.

Finishing

Join shoulder seams using 3-needle bind-off.

Using 16'' (40cm) circular needle, pick up neck stitches and work K1P1 rib for 6 rounds. Bind off all stitches.

Sew sleeve seams and set in sleeves.

Knitter's Comment:

If you like fast and easy knitting and working with lots of colors, resulting in an awesome sweater, this is the one. It takes 4 yards (3.6m) to knit around the front and back, so you may cut the yarns ahead if desired. Yarn changes may take place at any point, which is preferable to eliminate a bulky seam on one side.

The sleeves can be worked on circular needles from top to cuff as follows: starting at underarm, place marker, pick up 76 stitches around armhole with larger size 16'' (40cm) circular needle. Knit 2'' (5cm) then decrease 1 stitch each side of marker every inch (2.5 cm) 14 times. Change to double-point needles and decrease 6 stitches (42 stitches). Work K1P1 ribbing for 2'' (5cm) and bind off all stitches.

—Barbara Klein

Elaine's Comment:

This is one of my favorite sweaters to knit because I never get bored. I dye one skein of hand-painted yarn and go from there. Find a tide pool or some lupines for inspiration and make up your own palette. The hand-painted yarn brings the whole project together, as it integrates many colors in one skein, and that can be the basis to find individual colors to add to the mix and bring harmony to the project.

■ TOP-DOWN RAGLAN PULLOVER

Easy to knit while on the go!

MATERIALS AND NEEDLES

2 (2, 3) skeins hand-painted worsted weight yarn, 4 oz (114g), 250 yds (230m)

16'' (40cm) & 24'' (60cm) circular needles, size 8 (5mm; Can/UK size 6), or size needed to match gauge

GAUGE: 18 stitches = 4'' (10cm)

FINISHED CHEST MEASUREMENTS: 22 (24, 26)'' [56 (61, 66)cm]

DIRECTIONS FOR SIZE 2 (4, 6) YEARS.

WORK INSTRUCTIONS

Body

With 16'' (40cm) circular needle, cast on 68 stitches. Join round, being careful not to twist stitches. Knit every round for 1½'' (3.5cm). Begin raglan increases as follows:

1ST INCREASE ROUND: increase 1 stitch by knitting in the front and back of stitch, put marker on needle, increase 1, knit 22 (front), increase 1, place marker, increase 1, knit 8 (sleeve), increase 1, place marker, increase 1, knit 22 (back), increase 1, place marker, increase 1, knit 8 (sleeve). Total on needle: 76 stitches.

ROUND 2: Knit.

Continue working rounds 1 & 2, increasing 1 stitch before and after each marker (8 stitches added) every other round until raglan shaping measures approximately 5 (6, 7)'' [12.5 (15.5, 18)cm] or 162 (170, 186) stitches, changing to longer needle when desired.

For a rolled cuff, work in stockinette stitch until sleeve measures 8 (9, 10)" [20 (22.75, 25.25)cm] or desired length. Bind off all stitches.

If ribbing is desired instead of a rolled cuff, knit until sleeve is 7 (8, 9)" [18 (20, 23)cm], and work ribbing for 1" (2.5 cm). Bind off all stitches.

Finishing

Sew sleeve seams.

Knitter's Comment:

This sweater is really a no-brainer—simple, simple, simple! It is a great weekend project. Noro yarn is yummy to work with. I have also made it with Cestari cotton and wool, which is more practical for an everyday sweater. Warning: this may make you want to have another baby!

—Diane Joannides

Elaine's Comment:

This is an easy sweater for the new mother who is also a beginner knitter. You can hand-paint some yarn for the project or use any yarn that gives you the gauge required. When changing to a new skein of hand-painted yarn, alternate 2 rows of the old skein and 2 rows of the new skein to help the yarns blend together if they are a little different.

Divide for Body and Sleeves

Knit front stitches to marker, put stitches for 1st sleeve on holder, cast on 2 stitches for underarm, knit back stitches, put 2nd sleeve stitches on holder, cast on 2 stitches.

For a rolled edge, continue knitting until body measures 8 (9, 10)" [20.5 (23, 25.5)cm] from underarm. Bind off all stitches.

If ribbing is desired instead of a rolled edge, knit until body is 7 (8, 9)" [18 (20, 23)cm] from underarm, then work ribbing for 1" (2.5 cm).

Sleeves

With 16" (40cm) circular needle, pick up stitches from holder, increase 1 stitch each side for underarm. Do not join round; the sleeves are worked back and forth.

■ ZIGZAG PILLOW

Every stitch adds color and harmony to this pillow.

MATERIALS AND NEEDLES

Contrast color (CC): 1 skein hand-painted
   worsted weight yarn, 4 oz (114g),
   250 yds (230m)

Main color (MC): 2 skeins Brown Sheep
   Company worsted weight wool,
   4 oz (114g), 190 yds (174 m) each

Single-point needles, size 8 (5mm; Can/UK
   size 6), or size needed to match gauge

16" (40.5cm) pillow form

FINISHED MEASUREMENTS: 16" (40.5cm) square

GAUGE: 18 stitches = 4" (10cm)

WORK INSTRUCTIONS

Pattern stitch (multiple of 11 stitches):

ROWS 1–5: Knit in main color (MC).

ROW 6: (right side) With CC, K2 together, K2, knit into front and back of each of the next 2 stitches. K 3, slip 1, K1, psso. Repeat to end of row.

ROW 7: Purl.

ROWS 8–11: Repeat rows 6 & 7.

ROW 12: With MC, repeat row 6.

The zigzag pattern not only makes a handsome pillow, it is perfect for an afghan. This richly colored throw is one of my favorite knitted creations ever.

Front

Cast on 77 stitches in MC. Work 10 rows of garter stitch. Begin pattern stitch, starting row 6 and continue working the 12-row pattern repeat until piece measures approximately 16" (40.5cm), ending with 10 rows of MC garter stitch border.

Back

Work same as front.

Finishing

Sew up pillow on 3 sides, insert pillow form, and sew up last edge.

Knitter's Comment:

This pillow was fun and easy! Elaine has proven that colors do not have to coordinate while in the skein to look great together when knitted!

—Diane Joannides

Elaine's Comment:

Using hand-painted yarn makes this pillow interesting in color and texture. Every stitch will bring in a new color and fascinate the knitter who has also dyed the yarn. Great fun to make as a gift. You can also make this pillow using leftovers of hand-painted and other dyed yarns, allowing for colorful changes.

PHOTOGRAPH BY NANCE TRUEWORTHY

■ WINTER SHAWL

A great accent for a cold evening

MATERIALS AND NEEDLES

24 oz (681g) assorted dyed worsted weight
yarns (silk, mohair, wool, boucle)

35'' (89cm) circular needle, size 9 (5.5mm;
Can/UK size 5), or size needed to
match gauge

FINISHED MEASUREMENTS: 60'' by 24'' (152cm
by 61cm)

GAUGE: 14 stitches = 4'' (10cm)

WORK INSTRUCTIONS

This piece is worked sideways in bands of assorted yarns.

With your first yarn choice, cast on 210 stitches.
Working back and forth, work 6 rows of stockinette
stitch.

Change to the next kind of yarn and work 6 rows
of reverse stockinette (the purl side faces you).

Continue making bands with assorted yarns. This
will form a beautifully textured shawl.

When piece measures approximately 24'' (61cm)
when spread out flat, and the last panel is complete, bind off all stitches loosely.

Fringe

To make an 8'' (20.25cm) fringe, cut 16'' (40.5cm)
strands of different yarns and knot along both ends
of shawl as described on page 101 in the directions
for the Textured Scarf.

(For a very full fringe such as shown here, attach
4 strands at a time, knotting two 4-strand bundles
into each pattern band.)

Knitter's Comment:

This shawl can be knit using mixed yarns that were dyed in the same dye pot. You can overdye some old yarns that need a new home or use different textures that start out white. The pattern is easy to do and can use many textures for any adventurous knitter.

—Sage Eskesen

Elaine's Comment:

I love making this shawl because the textures are so inviting to experiment with. Using natural yarns, the textures shine as each new fiber finds a distinction with the knitted stitch.

■ SAMPLER VEST

Lots of textures give this vest some zip!

MATERIALS AND NEEDLES

Main color (MC): 1 skein dyed sport weight
   yarn, 4 oz (114g), 350 yds (320m)
Sampler colors: 10 hanks of various yarns (silk,
   boucle, mohair), 2 oz (57g) each
36'' (91.5cm) circular needles, size 5 & 7
(3.75mm & 4.5mm; Can/UK sizes 9 & 7)
Double-point needles, size 5 (3.75mm;
   Can/UK size 9)
5 buttons, ½'' (10mm)

FINISHED CHEST MEASUREMENTS: 36 (40, 42)''
[91.5 (101.5, 106.5)cm]

GAUGE: in stockinette stitch, 18 stitches = 4''
(10cm) on size 7 (4.5mm; Can/UK size 7) needles,
or size needed to match gauge

WORK INSTRUCTIONS

Body

With smaller circular needle and MC, cast on 162
(180, 190) stitches. Do NOT join round; this vest is
worked back and forth. Work in seed stitch (K1P1
for 1 row, then P1K1 on the next row, repeat these
2 rows).

On third row, begin 1st buttonhole: K1P1 in seed
stitch, knit next 2 stitches and slip 1st knit stitch
over 2nd knit stitch and off right needle, put remaining knit stitch back on left needle and knit together
with next stitch. Continue in established seed stitch
pattern to end of row.

FOURTH ROW: work seed stitch to last 2 stitches,
cast on 2 stitches over buttonhole, work seed stitch
for last 2 stitches.

PHOTOGRAPH BY NANCE TRUEWORTHY

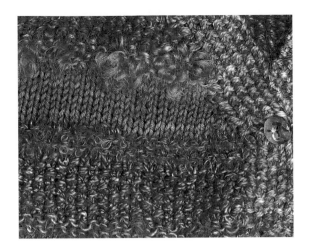

Continue working seed stitch for 1½" (3.8cm). Put first 6 and last 6 stitches on small stitch holders for front left and right bands (to be finished later).

Change to larger needle and another choice of yarn and begin pattern sequence for vest.

PATTERN SEQUENCE: With first sampler yarn, work in stockinette stitch (knit one row, purl one row) for 8 rows. With new yarn, work 4 rows of garter stitch (knit every row). Change yarn and work 8 rows of seed stitch. Change yarn again and work 4 rows of garter stitch.

Continue to change yarns and follow the sequence of stockinette stitch, garter stitch, seed stitch, and garter stitch until the piece measures 12 (13, 14)" [30.5 (33, 35.5)cm] or desired length to armhole.

Divide for front and back: work pattern for 38 (42, 44) stitches, bind off 6 stitches for underarm, and work to end of row. Next row, work 38 (42, 44) stitches for front, bind off 6 stitches and work remaining stitches for the back. Put front stitches on holders.

Back

Continue working on back in established pattern, decreasing 1 stitch at armhole edge of every other row 3 times. Work until armhole measures 9 (9, 10)" [23 (23, 25.5)cm]. Put back stitches on a holder.

Front

Pick up front stitches and work in established pattern as on the back, decreasing at armhole edge. At the same time, begin front V-neck shaping by decreasing 1 stitch at each neck edge, every other row, until 20 (24, 26) stitches remain. Work even until front measures same as back. Keep all stitches on the needle.

Finishing

Join shoulders by working 3-needle bind-off.

With MC and double-point needles, pick up button band stitches from holder on left front. Work front band in seed stitch, attaching band to garment by picking up a stitch at garment edge and knitting it together with the adjacent front-band stitch. Work to the middle of back neck and put stitches on a holder.

Pick up buttonhole band stitches from right front holder and work the same way as button band, making four more buttonholes as described above, approximately 3" (7.5cm) apart. When this 2nd band reaches the center neck, join bands using 3-needle bind-off.

Align buttons on left band and sew in place.

■ KID'S RIBBED PULLOVER

A bouncy sweater for an active child

MATERIALS AND NEEDLES

1 skein Brown Sheep Company sport weight wool, 4 oz (114g), 350 yds (320m)

1 skein Avalon silk, 3.5 oz (100g), 220 yds (200m)

1 skein Ballerina nylon, 4 oz (114g), 225 yds (206m)

16'' (40cm) and 24'' (60cm) circular needles, size 6 (4mm; Can/UK size 8), or size needed to match gauge

Straight needles, size 6 (4mm; Can/UK size 8)

FINISHED CHEST MEASUREMENTS: 22 (24, 26)'' [56 (61, 66)cm]

GAUGE: 20 stitches = 4'' (10cm)

WORK INSTRUCTIONS

Body

With 24'' (60cm) circular needle, cast on 120 (130, 140) stitches with 1-ply yarn, and join round, being careful not to twist stitches. Work in stockinette stitch (knit every round) for 8 rounds.

Change to next yarn texture (Ballerina), and start reverse stockinette stitch (purl on right side). **TIP:** When changing texture from a band of knit rounds to a band of purl rounds, make sure that the first round is knit with the new texture, so that the first round of purled stitches isn't half old texture and half new texture.

Purl for 6 rounds. Change to the 3rd texture (silk) and work 8 rows of stockinette.

Continue working the knit and purl ribs with the three-texture sequence, until piece measures 7 (8, 9)'' [18 (20.5, 23)cm] when slightly stretched. The rib will look scrunched up due to the nature of the pattern; you can decide to block it later, but remember to take this into account as you measure the garment.

Divide for Front and Back

At the beginning of next round, bind off 4 stitches for underarm, work 56 (61, 66) stitches, bind off 4 stitches and work remaining stitches.

Back

Put front stitches on a holder and work back in established pattern until piece measures 11½ (13, 15)" [29 (33, 38) cm]. Put these stitches on holder.

Front

Pick up front stitches and work in pattern until piece measures 9 (11, 13)" [23 (28, 33) cm].

Neck shaping: knit 17 (19, 22) stitches, put 22 stitches on a small holder, add a new ball of yarn and knit to end of row. Work both sides, decreasing 1 stitch at each neck edge, every other row, 3 times. Continue until front measures same as back. Keep the stitches on the needle.

Sleeves

With straight needles, cast on 34 (36, 38) stitches, using the same yarn as on the body of the sweater. Work the 8 rows of stockinette stitch (knit 1 row, purl 1 row when working flat). Continue in established pattern, increasing 1 stitch at each edge of every 4th row 6 (7, 11) times—46 (50, 60) stitches total.

Work until sleeve measures 7 (8, 10)" [17.75 (20.25, 25.5) cm] or desired length. Bind off all stitches loosely.

Finishing

Join shoulder seams using 3-needle bind-off.

With 16" (40cm) circular needle, pick up all neck stitches and knit for 6 rounds. Bind off loosely.

Sew sleeve seams and sew sleeve in place.

Knitter's Comment:

This was a lot easier than it looked! The textured yarn and the subtle color contrast kept the knitting interesting, and the color was absolutely stunning. Any little kid would feel like a star in this pullover. At my weekly knitting group, everybody wanted to touch it and wondered whose yarn it was. I had not worked with silk before, what a treat! The perky little ribs inspired me to use the same technique on the skirt of a little dress for my granddaughter, Chloe. She loves the bounciness!

Tip: *Carrying the yarns up the inside, when changing colors, eliminates sewing in all those loose ends, which can be tough with textured yarns. Just be sure to catch them with the yarn in use every other row, to avoid long floats that snag little fingers.*

—Carol Aigner Bacon

Elaine's Comment:

This is a wonderful little sweater to try new yarns you've dyed. Even though the skeins are all dyed together, the textures dye differently, so the color has subtle variations. I like the simplicity of the color/texture changes. You could add more texture or colors. This sweater can also easily be made in an adult version.

Glossary

Acid dye: A dye that is a salt of an organic acid. Acid is required as a dyeing assistant to set the dye to the fiber. The class of dye used for protein fibers.

Adjacent: Colors that lie next to one another on the color wheel, such as red and red-orange.

Aggressive colors: Warm colors, such as red, orange, and yellow.

Analogous colors: Colors that are closely related and near one another on the color wheel, usually within a quarter section of the wheel.

Cellulose fiber: Plant fibers, such as cotton and linen.

Chemical assist: A chemical used with a specific dye to aid in the dye process.

Color wheel: A circular chart showing the color spectrum and color relationships.

Complement: The color that is directly opposite another on the color wheel; orange is the complement of blue.

Depth of shade: The value of a color. Determined by the relationship between the weight of the fiber being dyed and the amount of dye used.

Diffusion: The movement of dye molecules in the dye bath.

Dye: A substance used to change the color of a fiber.

Dye bath: A pot of water to which dye and mordant have been added.

Dye formula: The proportions of colors to mix together to form a particular color.

Dye stock solution: A solution of a specific amount of dye dissolved in a measured amount of water, often expressed as a percentage.

Exhaust dyeing: The procedure in dyeing when the fiber is immersed in a dye bath and all or most of the dye molecules attach to the fibers.

Exhaust: The movement and absorption of the dye from the dye bath to the fiber.

Fastness: The ability of a dye to resist fading and stay the same color once it's on the fiber.

Felting: The shrinking and matting together of fibers when they are subjected to moisture, sudden temperature changes, and agitation. An undesirable result when it happens in the dye bath.

Fiber-reactive dye: A synthetic dye used with cellulose fibers, using salt and alkali as dyeing assistants.

Fixation: The point in the dye process when the dye molecules bond to the fiber.

Gram (g): The metric unit of weight. 1 gram = 0.035 ounce. 1 ounce = 28.35 grams.

Hue: The name of a color, such as red or green.

Ikat: Tie-dyeing technique, a wrapped resist, that creates a colorful and unusual pattern in the warp or weft when the dyed fiber is woven into fabric.

Immersion dyeing: The process in which the yarn is submerged in a dye pot that contains water, dye, and a chemical assistant (mordant).

Intensity: See *Saturation*.

Intermediate color: A color produced by combining a primary color and an adjacent secondary color on the color wheel.

Leveling: The process by which the dye is evenly distributed on the dyed fiber.

Lightfastness: The ability of a dye to maintain its color when exposed to sunlight.

Liter: The metric unit of volume. 1 liter = 33.8 ounces; 1 quart = 0.946 liter.

Meter: The metric unit of length. 1 meter = 39.37 inches; 1 yard = 0.914 meter.

Mordant: A chemical, such as citric acid, that helps set the dye in the fiber.

Overdyeing: Re-dyeing previously dyed yarn to alter the original color.

Palette: Colors selected to dye yarns, ranging from warm to cool.

Primary color: Colors that cannot be mixed from any other. The primaries are red, yellow, and blue.

Protein fiber: A fiber, such as wool, produced by an animal.

Receding colors: Cool colors on the color wheel, such as green, blue, and violet.

Saturation: Also called intensity. The amount of pure color in a hue; the higher the color saturation, the brighter the color.

Secondary color: A color that is mixed using two primary colors: orange, violet, and green.

Shade: Variations of a color made by adding black. A color can also be made darker by adding its complement.

Split complement: The colors on each side of a color's opposite on the color wheel: orange has blue-violet and blue-green as split complements.

Steaming: Heating fiber without immersion. Used to set the dye when hand-painting yarn.

Tint: A variation of a color made by adding white. In dyeing, where white cannot be added, less dye is used to achieve a tint.

Tone: A color plus gray. In dyeing, a tone can also be made by adding a small amount of a color's complement to the tint of a color.

Unfixed dye: Dye that has not bonded to the fiber in the dye bath.

Value: The lightness or darkness of a color when compared to a scale of grays ranging from black to white.

Washfastness: A dye's ability to maintain its color when washed.

Wetting out: The process of soaking the fiber in water before dyeing to allow the dye to penetrate the yarn evenly.

KNITTING ABBREVIATIONS

CC: contrast color

cm: centimeter; centimeters

g: gram

garter stitch: knit every row

K1P1: knit 1, purl 1 (a ribbing)

K2P2: knit 2, purl 2 (a ribbing)

K2 together: knit 2 stitches together (a decrease)

m: meter; meters

MC: main color

oz: ounces

psso: pass slipped stitch over

seed stitch: Row 1—knit 1, purl 1. Row 2—knit the purl stitches and purl the knit stitches.

slip 1: slip a stitch to right needle without knitting it

stockinette stitch: knit one row, purl one row

yds: yards

YO: yarn over, wrapping yarn over the needle to make a stitch

*: symbol to indicate a step in knitting directions that will be repeated one or more times

Bibliography

ART AND INSPIRATION

Bacci, Mina. *Leonardo*. New York: Avenel Books, 1978.

Becks-Malorny, Ulrike. *Paul Cézanne 1839–1906: Pioneer of Modernism*. Köln, Germany: Benedikt Taschen Verlag GmbH & Co., 1995.

Brafford, C.J., and Laine Thom. *Dancing Colors: Paths of Native American Women*. San Francisco: Chronicle Books, 1992.

Bumpus, Judith. *Van Gogh's Flowers*. London: Phaidon Press, 1998.

Callaway, Nicholas, ed. *Georgia O'Keeffe: One Hundred Flowers*. New York: Alfred A. Knopf, 1987.

Cameron, Julia, with Mark Bryan. *The Artist's Way: A Spiritual Path to Higher Creativity*. New York: G. P. Putnam's Sons, 1992.

Cooper, Frank M. *Oriental Carpets in Miniature*. Loveland, CO: Interweave Press, 1994.

Cowart, Jack, and Juan Hamilton. *Georgia O'Keeffe: Art and Letters*. Washington, DC: National Gallery of Art, 1987.

de Vecchi, Pierluigi. *Michelangelo*. New York: Henry Holt and Co., 1990.

Dendel, Esther Warner. *Designing From Nature: A Source Book for Artists and Craftsmen*. New York: Taplinger Publishing Co., 1978.

Duchting, Hajo. *Wassily Kandinsky 1866–1944: A Revolution in Painting*. Köln, Germany: Benedikt Taschen Verlag GmbH & Co, 1991.

Durozoi, Gerard. *Matisse: The Masterworks*. New York: Portland House, 1989

Ferris, Scott R., and Ellen Pearce. *Rockwell Kent's Forgotten Landscapes*. Camden, ME: Down East Books, 1998.

Flam, Jack, ed. *Matisse: A Retrospective*. New York: Park Lane, 1988.

Goldsmith, Lawrence C. *Watercolor Bold and Free: 64 Experimental Techniques in Watercolor*. New York: Watson-Guptill Publications, 2000.

Goldsworthy, Andy. *Andy Goldsworthy: A Collaboration with Nature*. New York: Harry N. Abrams, 1990.

Grasset, Eugene. *Art Nouveau: Floral Designs*. London: Bracken Books, 1988.

Jerstorp, Karin, and Eva Kohlmark. *The Textile Design Book*. Asheville, NC: Lark Books, 1986.

Kalir, Jane. *Gustav Klimt: 25 Masterworks*. New York: Harry N. Abrams, 1989.

Klein, Kathryn, ed. *The Unbroken Thread: Conserving the Textile Traditions of Oaxaca*. Los Angeles: The Getty Conservation Institute, 1997.

Lewison, Jeremy. *Anish Kapoor: Drawings*. London: Tate Gallery Publications, 1990.

Messent, Jan. *Design Sources for Pattern*. Wilts: Redwood Books, 1992.

Mowry, Elizabeth. *The Pastelist's Year: Painting the Four Seasons in Pastel*. New York: Watson-Guptill Publications, 2001.

Naubert-Riser, Constance. *Klee: The Masterworks*. London: Bracken Books, 1988.

O'Keeffe, Georgia. *Georgia O'Keeffe*. New York: Viking Press, 1976.

Rothenstein, Sir John. *The Moderns and Their World*. London: Phoenix House, 1957.

Orr, Lynn Federle, Paul Hayes Tucker, and Elizabeth Murray. *Monet: Late Paintings of Giverny from the Musee Marmottan*. San Francisco: Fine Arts Museum of San Francisco, 1994.

Pedretti, Carlo. *Leonardo da Vinci: Nature Studies from the Royal Library at Windsor Castle*. Royal Academy of Arts, 1981.

Petrie, Flinders. *Decorative Patterns of the Ancient World*. New York: Crescent Books, 1990.

Sark. *Succulent Wild Woman: Dancing wth Your Wonder-Full Self!* New York: Fireside Books, 1997.

Sayer, Chloe. *Arts and Crafts of Mexico*. San Francisco: Chronicle Books, 1990.

Scamuzzi, Ernesto. *Egyptian Art: In the Egyptian Museum of Turin*. New York: Harry N. Abrams, 1965.

Stuckey, Charles F., ed. *Monet: A Retrospective*. New York: Park Lane, 1985.

Tate Gallery. *Mark Rothko 1903–1970*. New York: Stewart, Tabori and Chang, 1996.

Tériade, E. "Matisse Speaks." *Art News*, Nov. 1951.

Watkins, Nicholas. *Bonnard*. London: Phaidon Press, 1994.

Weiss, Jeffrey, ed. *Mark Rothko*. New Haven & London: Yale Univ. Press, 1998.

White, Barbara Ehrlich. *Renoir: His Life, Art and Letters*. New York: Harry N. Abrams, 1984.

COLOR

Birren, Faber. *Principles of Color*. West Chester, PA: Schiffer Publishing, 1987.

———. *The Power of Color*. Secaucus, NJ: Carol Publishing Group, 1992.

Chevreul, M.E. *The Principles of Harmony and Contrast of Colors and Their Applications to the Arts*. West Chester, PA: Schiffer Publishing, 1981.

Color Sourcebook. Rockport, MA: Rockport Publishers, 1989.

Heline, Corinne. *Healing and Regeneration through Color*. Santa Barbara, CA: J.F. Rowny Press, 1964.

Itten, Johannes, *The Art of Color*. New York: Van Nostrand Reinhold, 1973.

———. *The Color Star*. New York: Van Nostrand Reinhold, 1985.

Leland, Nina. *Exploring Color*. Cincinnati, OH: North Light Books, 1998.

Menz, Deb. *Colorworks*, Loveland, CO. Interweave Press, 2004.

Shroyer, Nancy. *How to Select Color Palettes for Knitting and Other Fiber Arts: A Set of Formulas Specifically Developed for Use with a Color Wheel.* Cary, NC: Nancy's Knit Knacks LLC, 2001.

Walch, Margaret, and Augustine Hope. *Living Colors: The Definitive Guide to Color Palettes through the Ages.* San Francisco: Chronicle Books, 1995.

DYEING

Adrosko, Rita J. *Natural Dyes and Home Dyeing: A Practical Guide With Over 150 Recipes.* New York: Dover Publications, 1971.

Bemiss, Elijah. *The Dyer's Companion.* New York: Dover Publications, 1973.

Blumenthal, Betsy, and Kathryn Kreider. *Hands On Dyeing.* Loveland, CO: Interweave Press, 1988.

Davenport, Elsie G. *Your Yarn Dyeing.* Tarzana, CA: Select Books, 1976.

Davidson, Mary Frances. *The Dye-Pot.* Gatlinburg, TN: Mary Frances Davidson, 1991.

Grierson, Su. *Dyeing and Dyestuffs.* Haverfordwest, GB: Shire Publications, 1989.

Simmons, Max. *Dyes and Dyeing.* New York: Van Nostrand Reinhold, 1978.

Heath, Laurice. *Beautiful Wool: A Hand-Dyer's Guide.* Fredericksburg, TX: Cabin Ridge Press, 2002.

Knutson, Linda. *Synthetic Dyes and Natural Fibers.* Seattle, WA: Madrona Publishers, 1982.

Kolander, Cheryl. *A Silk Worker's Journal.* Loveland, CO: Interweave Press, 1979.

Ross, Nan Thayer. *Purple on Silk: A Shaker Eldress and Her Dye Journal.* New Gloucester, ME: United Society of Shakers, 2003.

Kramer, Jack. *Natural Plant Dyes & Processes.* New York: Charles Scribner's Sons, 1972.

Liles, J. N. *The Art and Craft of Natural Dyeing: Traditional Recipes for Modern Use.* Knoxville: Univ. of Tennessee Press, 1990.

Lincoln, Maryanne. *Recipes from the Dye Kitchen.* Harrisburg, PA: Rug Hooking, 1999.

McRae, Bobbi A. *Colors from Nature: Growing, Collecting, & Using Natural Dyes.* Pownal, VT: Storey Communications, 1993.

Morey, Nancy L. *Rainbow Dyeing: A Multi-Color Approach to Dyeing.* Binghamton, NY: All Ready, 1987.

Neel, Jean M. *I'd Rather Dye Laughing.* Petaluma, CA: Unicorn Books and Crafts, 1984.

Vinroot, Sally, and Jennie Crowder. *The New Dyer.* Loveland, CO: Interweave Press, 1981.

Wickens, Hetty. *Natural Dyes for Spinners and Weavers.* London: BT Batsford, 1983.

KNITTING

Epstein, Nicky. *Nicky Epstein's Knitted Embellishments.* Loveland, CO: Interweave Press, 1999.

Falick, Melanie. *Knitting in America: Patterns, Profiles, & Stories of America's Leading Artisans.* New York: Artisan, 1996.

Fassett, Kaffe. *Glorious Knits.* New York: Clarkson N. Potter, 1985.

———. *Kaffe Fassett's Glorious Inspiration for Needlepoint & Knitting.* New York: Sterling Publishing Co., 1991.

Feitelson, Ann. *The Art of Fair Isle Knitting.* Loveland, CO: Interweave Press, 1999.

Goldberg, Rhoda Ochser. *The New Knitting Dictionary.* New York: Crown Publishers, 1984.

Harmony Guide to Colourful Machine Knitting, The. London: Lyric Books, 1989.

Harmony Guide to Knitting Stitches, The. London: Lyric Books, 1983.

Harrell, Betsy. *Anatolian Knitting Designs.* Istanbul: Redhouse Press, 1981.

Hiatt, Beryl and Phelps, Linden. *Simply Beautiful Sweaters.* Bothell, WA: Martingale & Co., 1992.

Lydon, Susan Gordon. *The Knitting Sutra: Craft as a Spiritual Practice.* San Francisco: Harper, 1997.

Mapstone, Prudence. *Freeform: Serendipitous Design Techniques for Knitting & Crochet.* Brisbane, Australia: Prudence Mapstone, 2002.

Murphy, Bernadette. *Zen and the Art of Knitting.* Avon, MA: Adams Media Corporation, 2002.

Myers, Lisa R. *The Joy of Knitting.* Philadelphia: Running Press, 2001.

Nargi, Lela. *Knitting Lessons: Tales from the Knitting Path.* New York: Penguin Group, 2003.

Righetti, Maggie. *Sweater Design in Plain English.* New York: St. Martin's Press, 1990.

Roghaar, Linda, and Molly Wolf, eds. *Knit Lit: Sweaters and Their Stories . . . and Other Writing About Knitting.* New York: Three Rivers Press, 2002.

Rush, Helene, and Rachel Emmons. *Sweaters by Hand.* Loveland, CO: Interweave Press, 1988.

Square, Vicki. *The Knitter's Companion.* Loveland, CO: Interweave Press, 1996.

Starmore, Alice. *Alice Starmore's Book of Fair Isle Knitting.* Newtown, CT: Taunton Press, 1988.

———. *Charts for Colour Knitting.* Achmore, Isle of Lewis: Windfall Press, 1992.

Sundbo, Annemor. *Everyday Knitting: Treasures From a Ragpile.* Kristiansand, Norway: Torridal Tweed, 1994.

Upitis, Lisbeth. *Latvian Mittens,* St. Paul, MN: Dos Tejedoras, 1981.

Vogel, Lynne. *The Twisted Sisters Sock Workbook.* Loveland, CO: Interweave Press, 2002.

Walker, Barbara. *Charted Knitting Designs: A Third Treasury of Knitting Patterns.* Pittsville, WI: Schoolhouse Press, 1972

Williams, Joyce. *Latvian Dreams: Knitting from Weaving Charts.* Pittsville, WI: Schoolhouse Press, 2000.

Zilboorg, Anna. *45 Fine & Fanciful Hats to Knit.* Asheville, NC: Lark Books, 1997.

———. *Simply Socks.* Asheville, NC: Lark Books, 2000.

Zimmerman, Elizabeth. *Knitting Around,* Pittsville, WI: Schoolhouse Press, 1989.

Suppliers

These are sources of dyeing supplies and yarns that I use. Some are wholesale only, but can direct you to a store near you that carries their products.

Pro Chemical and Dye
P.O. Box 14
Somerset MA 02726
1-800-2-BUY-DYE
www.prochemical.com
(Dyes and dye equipment)

Brown Sheep Company
100662 County Road 16
Mitchell NE 69357-9748
1-800-826-9136
www.brownsheep.com
(1-ply and 2-ply wool yarns)

Chester Farms
3581 Churchville Ave.
Churchville VA 24421
1-877-ONE-WOOL
www.chesterfarms.com
(2-ply ragg wool yarn)

Green Mountain Spinnery
P.O. Box 568
Putney VT 05346
1-800-321-9665
www.spinnery.com
(2-ply gray ragg wool yarn)

Henry's Attic
5 Mercury Avenue
Monroe NY 10950-9736
1-845-783-0482
(Silk, Ballerina, Texas, and Mikado yarns)

Louet Sales
808 Commerce Park Drive
Ogdensburg NY 13669
1-800-897-6444
www.louet.com
(Le Bouffon Thick-and-Thin bulky wool yarn)

Pine Tree Yarns
P.O. Box 506
Damariscotta ME 04543
1-207-563-8909
www.pinetreeyarns.com
(Dye sampler kits, yarns, and sweater kits to dye)

Index